S
A
L
T
      P
T
      E
      P
      P
      E
      R

SALT &

CHRONICLE BOOKS

SAN FRANCISCO

PEPPER

THE COOKBOOK

BY SANDRA COOK, SARA SLAVIN & DEBORAH JONES

PHOTOGRAPHS: DEBORAH JONES RECIPES AND FOOD STYLING: SANDRA COOK
ART DIRECTION AND STYLING: SARA SLAVIN TEXT: CAROLYN MILLER

Library of Congress Cataloging-in-Publication Data available.
ISBN 0-8118-3423-9
Manufactured in China.

Art direction and styling by Sara Slavin, Food styling by Sandra Cook,
Designed by Louise Fili and Mary Jane Callister/Louise Fili Ltd.
Cover photograph by Deborah Jones

Distributed in Canada by
RAINCOAST BOOKS
9050 Shaughnessy Street, Vancouver, BC V6P 6E5
10 9 8 7 6 5 4 3 2 1

CHRONICLE BOOKS LLC
85 Second Street, San Francisco, California 94105
www.chroniclebooks.com

Like water, like air, they seem givens in our life, yet for almost as long as time itself, salt and pepper have been substances of desire. Salt came first, the need and yearning for it stretching back even before the invention of language. Then, the earliest people followed animal tracks to salt outcroppings or springs, or gathered it from lagoons by the sea, for they knew that these glistening crystals added something to food that nothing else could provide: savor, that sparkling expansion of taste on the tongue.

The longing for salt is more basic than just the flavor it brings out in food, as the human body needs salt to regulate its fluids, especially when our natural salt level is depleted by heat or exercise. Like the oceans, our blood is salty, for we came from the sea, the salty water of life that once covered almost everything, and we still need to go back to it, sprinkling its crystallized essence into our food.

So central are they to cuisine that the course of civilization can be charted by the search for salt and its companion, pepper, which adds another kind of spark to food: a sharp, spicy heat. Trade routes were established, cities were founded, and new continents were discovered in the urge to satisfy the taste for a crystallized mineral and the dried berries of the pepper vine.

Over the centuries, a cuisine evolved that depended on salt and pepper for more than just added flavor or piquancy. Salt, from the beginning, was highly valued as a preservative, as it was found that foods buried in salt or suspended in salt brine magically did not decay, but instead took on new taste and texture and lasted a long time. Thanks to this property of salt, we have sausages, hams, bacon, salt cod, olives, sauerkraut, pickles, preserved lemons, caviar, and *kimchee*. Salt is even used as a baking medium, sealing in flavor and moisture for fish, meats, vegetables, and fruits. Pepper has its own small branch of cookery: peppered meat and fish dishes, in which the spice forms a crust or a light coat surrounding the meat, and certain cheeses and highly flavored preserved meats.

And then there is the combination of the two properties—savor and heat—that through a marvelous synergy yields more than the sum of their parts, each bringing out the best in the other and heightening the flavor of any food they season. Although they seem like such simple ingredients, salt and pepper transform food and are the soul of cuisine.

Today, the obsession with ingredients that has revolutionized cooking in this country extends to salt and pepper, for we now know that various kinds of each yield subtle differences in taste and texture, and that the kind of salt used should depend on how it is used. Instead of just the familiar blue Morton's salt canister, we have the big red-and-white Diamond Crystal kosher salt box and a tall cylinder of sea salt. More and more, we're also likely to have small jars of sea salt — oyster-colored *sel gris*, or opaque, irregular crystals of *fleur de sel*, to sprinkle over green salads or sliced tomatoes, or to offer at the table. And a whole new range of specialty salts is opening up to satisfy our need for new flavors, colors, and textures: Hawaiian red clay or black lava salt, smoked Danish salt, pink Peruvian salt.

The choice of peppers expanded several years ago, with the increasing availability of white, pink, and green, each with its own special culinary niche (though technically, pink peppercorns, prized for their color and their crunchy texture, are not really pepper). Now we can even choose among different varieties of black and white pepper, from Malabar and Tellicherry to Sarawak.

In the pages that follow, you will find a collection of recipes that use salt and pepper both as basic ingredients and as the final perfecting touches that make all the difference in the success of a dish. We include glossaries of the unique kinds of salt and pepper available today, and a selection of secrets for how to use them for what they do better than any other ingredients: bring out the essential taste of good food in all its earthly beauty.

LAVENDER SALT ROSEMARY SALT MARGARITA WITH LIME SALT LIME SALT

RED SANDWICH MELON SALAD WITH LAVENDER SALT VINAIGRETTE SALT-ROASTED

POTATOES SALT-FRIED LIMA BEANS SALT CRACKERS SALT-BAKED WHOLE FISH

SALT-ROASTED SALMON SALAD WITH SALT-BRINED TROUT AND CITRUS VINAIGRETTE

ROASTED SAKE CRAB WITH SALT DIPPING SAUCE GRILLED SALTED CHICKEN LIVERS

AND RED ONION PRESERVED LEMONS AND ORANGES MOROCCAN-STYLE STEW

PEANUT BRITTLE WITH COARSE SALT SALTED ALMOND TUILES

Salt is the essence of the sea, the body of water that all life came from. Each cell of our body needs salt in order to function, and our blood has a salt content that almost exactly matches that of the ocean. It is hardly surprising, then, that as creatures of the sea, we should need to constantly replenish our bodies with salt, and that it should be an essential ingredient in the food we eat. We love salt for its own taste, one we first acquired from eating seafood gathered by the shore and from the uncooked flesh of animals. But we also love it for the particular magic that occurs when salt is added to other foods, causing their flavors to blossom fully and to unify in a finished dish. ✦ Salt comes from the residue of lost oceans and seas and from the evaporating edges of living ones, as well as from salt springs bubbling up out of the ground. The salt deposits found everywhere on our globe are the evaporated remains of bodies of saltwater that covered the land eons ago, and were then twisted by geologic movement into veins and pools that interlace the earth, balloon up into underground salt domes, and sometimes open out into the air. And in a similar way, salt has run through the unrecorded and recorded past of humans, such a constant companion that we can track the development of civilization and the creation of the modern world by its presence. ✦ The salt shaker we reach for so casually on our table is the result of millennia of human endeavor, laden with history, symbolism, and ritual. But our easy access to many varieties of salt is also a measure of the possibilities for our creature happiness, as food that is cooked and seasoned well is good not just for the body, but also for the soul. ✦ The recipes in this chapter illustrate a range of the uses of salt in the kitchen, from classic and time-honored to innovative and unexpected. Here, you will find recipes using salt to preserve foods, as in Preserved Lemons and Oranges; as a roasting medium to cook foods evenly and seal in moisture, as in Salt-Baked Whole Fish; to make a crust that protects and adds flavor to meat, as in Beef Tenderloin with Lavender Salt; and as a garnish, in recipes like Peanut Brittle with Coarse Salt or Margarita with Lime Salt. Flavored salts, such as Lavender Salt, Rosemary Salt, and Lime Salt, are heady concoctions to sprinkle on food as a garnish just before serving or to serve alongside it in small dishes at the table. All of the recipes in this chapter take advantage of the gift of salt to allow the flavor of food to bloom to its fullest.

Once humans learned to cook with fire, they had even more need and desire for the salt that they must have discovered when tracking animals to natural salt licks or salt springs or to the edge of the sea, for cooked meat loses some of the natural saltiness of uncooked flesh. One of the first steps toward civilization, then, involved not just cooking but seasoning food, and so we began our long march from survival toward culture: the development of those unnecessary acts and objects that lift life above mere existence. Salt became even more necessary once pottery was developed, for boiling meats in liquid leaches out a greater amount of their natural salt content than roasting. And once we began to cultivate and eat more grain, we, like the animals we domesticated by feeding them grain and providing them with salt, needed more of that substance ourselves.

The first trade routes were probably the tracks that migrating herds of grazing animals made, taking the way of least resistance, toward fresh pastures and salt. Humans followed, and once the animals were domesticated, both man and beast traveled the same routes. Animals were then used to carry trading goods to peoples in the mountains, and salt was one of the goods transported both ways.

Salt created empires for those people lucky enough to live near where they knew salt could be mined or gathered. The first was the Hallstatt empire of the Celts, whose riches were drawn from the extensive salt deposits of what is now Austria, and whose mines date back at least ten thousand years to the Neolithic era. The Hallstatt Celts traded with the Greeks, Egyptians, and the Romans, among others, and the abundance of their salt mines allowed them to spread through Europe and to colonize the British Isles.

Venice was the next great salt empire; it was salt from her lagoons that provided the wherewithal for that city to build ships and provide arms for the Crusades. The Crusaders, in return, awarded Venice the trading concessions they established in the Near East, making it the most important port through which spices (including pepper) entered Europe.

As long as salt was difficult to find, extract, and transport, it was taxed heavily by kings and governments, on the theory that since it was a product of the earth, and not created by men, it belonged to the state. Once the advances of the Industrial Revolution made it easier to process and ship salt, it lost much of its value as a commodity and instead became important for industrial uses: The two chemicals that make up salt, sodium and chloride, are the major ingredients in the production of plastics, chlorine bleach, dyes, paint, pharmaceuticals, and explosives.

THE VALUE OF SALT

Salt was once as important to civilization as oil is today, precious because it was so hard to extract and process, and because such large quantities were needed to sustain human populations, especially in cold climates, where people had to pickle meats and vegetables in order to have food during the long winters. Though salt is found in underground deposits in every country on earth except Japan (it is also somewhat rare in Scandinavia), it often had to be transported many miles from the salt mines to the populations who needed it. The importance of salt to civilization cannot be overestimated, for it was not only necessary in the cooking and preserving of food, but it was a major ingredient used in tanning leather, in smelting metal, and in making gunpowder, soap, glass, and pottery glazes. Salt was vital to settled peoples, and it was also the essential ingredient that made seagoing exploration and the expansion of empires possible. Salt cod was the food that powered the sailors not just of the ocean-crossing ships that discovered and claimed new worlds, but the first seagoing people, the Phoenicians who traveled the Mediterranean coasts; the salt cod dear to the cuisines of France, Italy, and Spain is their legacy. (Salt cod would grow in importance in the seventh century, when the Church forbade eating meat on Fridays.)

Rock salt was difficult to extract and expensive to transport due to its extreme weight, and the chunks of salt had to be broken into smaller chunks and then ground between stone wheels. So when the nobility sat at table, the salt cellar sat in the place of honor near the host, holding its dear substance. Those who sat near the host, or "above the salt," were in the place of honor; the seats "below the salt," far from arm's reach, were reserved for the less-fortunate relatives and hangers-on.

13

Not until the Industrial Revolution were means developed for the easy and inexpensive extraction and production of table salt. Mining was now replaced by the vacuum process still used today: Hot water is piped into the mines to dissolve the salt; the brine is then withdrawn and boiled to evaporate it. Once salt was no longer dear, and refrigeration replaced pickling and dry-salting as the means by which foods were preserved, it became "common" table salt, available to anyone for very little money. Now, when the preparation and enjoyment of food have achieved the level of art for many people in this country, and the traditional cuisines of other countries are being revived and refined, the ancient methods of harvesting sea salt are also being revived. Today, salt is farmed and harvested by hand from the edges of the sea, exactly as it was done millennia ago, in countries around the world. Gray sea salt is treasured for the slightly mineral taste it adds to cooked foods, and coarse grains of fleur de sel are sold in small boxes for sprinkling over food just as it is served. And thus salt, until so recently devalued and unappreciated, has again become a precious commodity in its natural form, rich with the flavor of the sea.

SALT VESSELS

The most important of the early containers devised to hold salt was the salting tub, a large stoneware container used to soak the large pieces of meat that had to be preserved over the winter. It's hard for us to understand today that at one time almost all food had to be either salted, dried, and/or smoked in order for it to last through the cold months, and that the quantities of salt needed for the salting tub were huge.

The earliest methods of extracting salt were backbreakingly difficult; it had to be mined with picks from pits and tunnels deep under the ground, and it emerged in blocks and chunks. The salt for brining and pickling in the salting tub could be used in large pieces, but salt cellars and spoons, salt grinders, and salt shakers evolved when ground and sea-harvested salt became more available. These coveted and prized salt accessories were symbols of a new level of sophistication and culture, and some, such as the salt cellars created by Cellini, reached the level of high art.

For the earliest peoples, salt was magic: A rock that dissolves in liquid yet keeps its essential salty taste, it can also reappear in the form of crystals when the liquid is evaporated. Because its essence never changes, and because it protects food from corruption, salt was seen as a pure material that could guard humans against other forms of evil. And because it was essential to humans for their food, for their domesticated grazing animals, and for the production of necessities like leather, the presence of salt was a guarantee that the culture would continue; this is no doubt the basis of the Salt Covenant between Jehovah and the Israelites. Salt was important in practical terms to the Jews, for they were originally vegetarians, and when they were allowed to eat meat, it was with the proviso that the blood had to be removed from it, which was done by salting.

Salt was important not only in the Jewish religion, but to the early Catholic church, whose baptismal ceremony for infants included placing a few grains of salt on the tongue of the child. This was undoubtedly a holdover from its importance as a purifying element in pagan religion, which used salt to drive out evil spirits and to guard against the possibility that they might reappear. Houses and sacred spaces were cleaned and protected by the sacrifice of a sprinkle of salt. And because salt was so costly, the gift of salt was also a token of hospitality, and anyone who accidentally spilled the precious crystals was considered unlucky and in danger of drawing the attention of evil spirits. The only remedy was to take a pinch of the spilled grains and throw them over your left shoulder, where all unseen malevolent forces were known to gather.

LAVENDER SALT

ABOUT ⅔ CUP

½ cup coarse sea salt

3 tablespoons dried lavender

Dip a tomato wedge into this salt blend, rub it on your beef tenderloin before roasting, or sprinkle it on roasted chicken or over vegetables.

Combine the sea salt and lavender in a small bowl and mix well. Store in an airtight container in a cupboard or pantry and use within 4 to 6 weeks.

ROSEMARY SALT

ABOUT ⅔ CUP

½ cup coarse sea salt

2 tablespoons chopped dried rosemary

Sprinkle this flavorful herb salt over tomato slices arranged on grilled bread, or over a pizza before slipping it into the oven.

Combine the sea salt and rosemary in a small bowl and mix well. Store in an airtight container in a cupboard or pantry and use within 4 to 6 weeks.

MARGARITA
WITH LIME SALT

1 cup superfine sugar

1 cup water

1 cup tequila

⅓ cup triple sec

2 cups fresh lime juice

¼ cup lime salt
(below)

ice cubes

A classic margarita, served on the rocks with a touch of lime salt.

In a large pitcher, dissolve the sugar in the water. Stir in the tequila, Triple Sec, and 1¾ cups of the lime juice. Pour the remaining ¼ cup lime juice into a shallow saucer. Pour the lime salt into a separate shallow saucer.

   Prepare the glasses by dipping the rim of each one first into the lime juice and then into the lime salt. Fill each glass with ice, pour in the margarita mix, and serve.

LIME SALT

½ cup kosher salt

2 tablespoons finely
grated lime zest

1 tablespoon fresh
lime juice

Lime salt is incredibly versatile, fragrant, and fresh tasting—the perfect salt for a margarita, for sprinkling on your favorite fish, or for adding to a vinaigrette recipe.

Combine the ingredients in a small bowl, mix well, and allow to dry out a bit before using, 20 to 30 minutes. Store in an airtight container in a cupboard or pantry and use within 3 days.

RED SANDWICH

SERVES 6

½ cup water

⅓ cup rice vinegar

1 small red onion, thinly sliced

4 tablespoons unsalted butter, at room temperature

6 slices dark rye or pumpernickel bread

3 beets, cooked, peeled, and thinly sliced

6 radishes, trimmed and thinly sliced

1 to 2 tablespoons fleur de sel

Fleur de sel completes an earthy, crisp, and piquant blend of texture and taste in this beautiful crimson open-faced sandwich. You can cut the sandwiches into small shapes for appetizers, or serve whole as a simple lunch.

In a small bowl, combine the water and rice vinegar. Place the onion slices in the bowl, cover, and refrigerate for about 30 minutes.

Drain the onion slices and pat dry. Butter the bread slices and layer each slice with the beets, radishes, and red onion. Sprinkle generously with fleur de sel and serve.

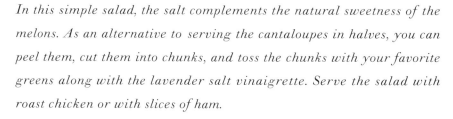

MELON SALAD
WITH LAVENDER SALT VINAIGRETTE

SERVES 4

¼ teaspoon lavender salt (page 16), plus extra salt for serving (optional)

1 teaspoon rice vinegar

2 teaspoons extra-virgin olive oil

2 tablespoons fresh tangerine or orange juice

1 tablespoon minced shallot

2 cantaloupes, cut in half, seeded, and chilled

In this simple salad, the salt complements the natural sweetness of the melons. As an alternative to serving the cantaloupes in halves, you can peel them, cut them into chunks, and toss the chunks with your favorite greens along with the lavender salt vinaigrette. Serve the salad with roast chicken or with slices of ham.

To make the vinaigrette, in a small bowl, mix together the ¼ teaspoon lavender salt, vinegar, olive oil, citrus juice, and shallot. Place the cantaloupe halves on individual plates and drizzle the vinaigrette evenly over them. Sprinkle with additional lavender salt, if desired.

SALT·ROASTED POTATOES

2 pounds small yukon gold or red potatoes, unpeeled

2 lemons, sliced about ½ inch thick

8 cloves garlic, peeled but left whole

2 tablespoons extra-virgin olive oil

2 tablespoons coarse gray sea salt

5 fresh rosemary sprigs

Something wonderful happens when you roast potatoes with lemon, garlic, rosemary, and salt. The lemons and garlic caramelize, the salt delivers flavor and a slight crunch, the potatoes become crisp and golden, and the rosemary scents everything.

Preheat the oven to 375°F.

In a large pot, combine the potatoes, lemon slices, and garlic with water to cover. Bring to a boil and cook until the potatoes are beginning to soften, about 45 to 50 minutes. Drain and transfer the potatoes, lemon slices, and garlic to a baking sheet. Drizzle with the olive oil and sprinkle with the sea salt. Toss lightly to coat evenly, then toss with the rosemary sprigs.

Bake, shaking the baking sheet once or twice to redistribute the potatoes and seasonings, until the potatoes are golden and tender, 35 to 40 minutes. Serve warm or at room temperature.

SALT-FRIED LIMA BEANS

S
E
R
V
E
S

4
T
O
6

vegetable oil for deep-frying

1 package (10 ounces) frozen lima beans, thawed

½ cup cornstarch

1 teaspoon kosher salt

½ teaspoon freshly ground black pepper

1 clove garlic

1 tablespoon fleur de sel or finishing salt of choice, plus extra salt for serving (optional)

These lima beans are a nearly addictive snack. It doesn't take long to cook them, so the scent of frying oil in your kitchen is minimal. A Microplane, a fine-screen stainless-steel grater, is ideal for finely shaving the garlic in this recipe. The fried beans can be kept in a warm oven for up to an hour before serving.

Line a baking sheet with paper towels. Pour vegetable oil to a depth of 2 inches into a skillet and heat over medium-high heat. Meanwhile, rinse the lima beans and drain; the beans should be slightly damp. In a shallow bowl, mix together the cornstarch, kosher salt, and black pepper. Toss the beans in the cornstarch mixture. Make sure they are well coated, then pour them into a colander and shake off the excess cornstarch. Finely shave (see recipe introduction) or mince the garlic and toss in a small dish with the fleur de sel, mixing well; set aside.

Test the temperature of the oil by dropping in a bean; if it sizzles and floats to the surface in seconds, the oil is ready. Working quickly, drop in the beans in small batches and stir constantly until lightly golden and crisp, about 1 minute. Remove with a slotted spoon to the prepared baking sheet to drain.

When all the beans are cooked, toss with the garlic-salt mixture. Sprinkle with additional salt, if desired, and serve warm.

SALT CRACKERS

- 2 cups all-purpose flour
- 3 tablespoons vegetable shortening
- 1½ teaspoons baking powder
- ½ teaspoon kosher salt
- 1½ teaspoons freshly ground black pepper
- ½ cup water
- 2 tablespoons extra-virgin olive oil
- 2 tablespoons coarse sea salt

More flavorful and with better texture than your average store-bought brand, these snappy little crackers are wonderful. We sprinkle Hawaiian sea salt on them, but you can choose your favorite flavored salt or coarse sea salt. Serve with soups, salads, topped with cheese, or with dips.

Preheat the oven to 350°F. Line a baking sheet with parchment paper.

Combine the flour, shortening, baking powder, kosher salt, and black pepper in a food processor. Process briefly to mix. Then, with the motor running, drizzle in the water. When the dough begins to hold together, turn off the processor.

Gather up the dough into a ball and transfer to a lightly floured work surface. Roll out into a sheet about ⅛ inch thick, and cut into 2-by-3-inch rectangles. Transfer the rectangles to the prepared baking sheet, then brush each rectangle lightly with olive oil and sprinkle with the coarse salt.

Bake until golden brown, 12 to 14 minutes. Let cool completely on the baking sheet on a wine rack. Store in an airtight container at room temperature for up to 1 week.

THE LOVE OF SALT

We love salty things: cheese, peanuts, pistachios, potato chips, tortilla chips, smoked oysters, anchovies (well, not everybody loves anchovies). Not only do we love them, but from time to time we crave them. Salty foods make us thirsty because our body always tries to equalize the level of salt it contains; when we lose salt and water through exercise, we need to add both water and salt to make up for that loss. When we eat salt, we need to drink liquid, so salty foods, which also pique the appetite, are natural appetizers to serve with drinks before dinner.

THE TASTE OF SALT

Sea salts, especially the unrefined ones, have a fuller, more complex taste than table salt, which can have a slightly bitter flavor, along with an aftertaste from the added iodine. Hand-gathered sea salt retains more minerals and more of the taste of the sea, and some of it is even faintly sweet. Specialty salts such as Hawaiian alae salt taste of the earth that colors them, and smoked and herbed salts taste of their added flavors. The general rule for specialty salts is to use the more assertively flavored ones with full-flavored foods. See the individual listings in the salt and pepper glossaries (pages 88–96) for more information on the taste of specific salts.

Some salts are saltier than others, simply because larger, unrefined grains take up more space in any given measure. For this reason, kosher salt is not as salty as table salt. One tablespoon of kosher salt equals about 2 teaspoons of table salt. Some coarse sea salt, however, can be saltier than the same amount of table salt, depending on the formation of the crystals. Taste a few grains of any kind of salt before adding it to food to judge taste and saltiness, and above all, remember to taste as you go, during each stage of preparing a dish.

KOSHER SALT VS. SEA SALT

Both kosher salt and sea salt have their advocates among chefs. American chefs tend to favor kosher salt, because it has no additives and because its large crystals are easier to pick up between the fingers; kosher salt is also quite inexpensive compared to sea salt. Many European chefs prefer their continent's sea salts, which have the added attraction of being available in both fine and coarse grains, and retain a faint mineral taste.

Most people who grew up in the United States in the middle of the last century knew only a few kinds of salt: Morton's in the round blue box; rock salt in bags if your family made ice cream or used rock salt to thaw the ice on their sidewalks; bottles of garlic salt or Lawry's seasoned salt (especially if your father liked to barbecue steaks); and a box of kosher salt, but only if your family was Jewish.

Today, the salt collection of anyone who loves to cook and eat is richer. The Morton's is still there, though its uses may be limited to cleaning copper, cleaning up spills, and being kept near the stove to smother any kitchen fires. The basics should include a fine sea salt for filling salt shakers; a salt box or covered bowl of kosher salt to add to pasta water in tablespoons and to foods and cooking water in pinches (and to use in large quantities for brines, salt crusts, and baking in salt); rock salt to use as a bed for stabilizing some foods (such as oysters on the half shell) during baking, and also for making ice cream if you use an electric or hand-cranked ice cream maker; fine or coarse sea salt in a container with a pour spout and holes for sprinkling as an alternative way of quickly seasoning food and cooking water; at least one kind of fleur de sel to sprinkle on salads, sliced tomatoes, and other dishes immediately before serving; and one or two other specialty salts for garnishing.

Some recipes tell you to salt food only at the end of cooking, but good cooks know that a pinch of salt should be added at the beginning of preparing any dish, even dried beans. The important things to remember are to taste as you go and to add a tiny pinch or sprinkle of salt at each stage of cooking. The recipes in this book, as in almost all cookbooks, should be considered just a guide; use your own palate to decide how much salt to add.

If a recipe calls for a specific amount of salt, use a little less than called for to make up for the salt you've added earlier, as well as to allow for the possibility that the dish may not need as much salt as the recipe specifies. Also, take care when the dish includes salty ingredients such as anchovies, Parmesan, or olives, or when it is cooked a long time so that the liquid is reduced, making it saltier. When adding salt to liquids and butter-based sauces, allow a moment or two for the salt to dissolve before tasting. Taste again before adding salt at the end of cooking; you may not need to add more.

WHEN NOT TO SALT

- Don't add salt when boiling corn on the cob, as it will toughen the kernels.
- Don't add salt when poaching, frying, or coddling eggs, for the salt will toughen the egg whites.
- Don't salt meat before sautéing or searing it; the salt will draw out the juices and keep the meat from browning as it should.
- Don't salt the water for poaching eggs, as it can keep the egg whites from setting properly.
- Some cooks believe that you should never salt meat before roasting or grilling, as the salt draws the juices out of the meat, although many others insist that this makes little difference and that the flavor added to the surface of the meat by seasoning before cooking outweighs any other concern.

THE USES OF SALT

Salt is the most important ingredient in the cook's pantry, for it brings out the flavor of other foods and unites all the disparate elements of a dish. But salt has many other uses in the kitchen, from making foods last longer to garnishing them on their way to the table.

PRESERVING The oldest use of salt, of course, is as simple flavoring for raw or cooked foods. But as soon as it was discovered that a layer of salt, or a salty solution, kept food from spoiling, this mineral became a necessity for anyone who had to transport food over long distances or preserve enough to last them through a hard winter. We have kept our taste for those kinds of foods; though we no longer need to salt, dry, and smoke our meat and vegetables, we still love bacon, sauerkraut, and sausages. And some foods, such as olives and the shells of citrus fruits, are edible only when their bitterness and toughness is transformed through interaction with salt, just as some flavorings, such as fish sauce and soy sauce, would not exist without salt. The three methods used for salt curing are brining, or immersing food in a salt-water solution; burying food in dry salt; and rubbing food with salt mixed with herbs, the classic method for making gravlax. Salt cures foods because it draws water, not just out of the cells of the foods themselves, but also from any cells of bacteria or mold that they might contain or attract; this inhibits the growth of the cells.

SALTING VEGETABLES Some recipes call for sliced eggplant, cucumber, and zucchini to be sprinkled or tossed with salt, then left to drain in a colander or on paper towels for 30 minutes or so; the salt is then brushed off with paper towels. This not only seasons the relatively bland vegetables somewhat, but draws out their slight bitterness as well as some of the moisture that can make them soggy when cooked or used in salads.

BLANCHING VEGETABLES Cooking vegetables briefly in salted boiling water until they are partially or fully cooked helps to bring out their color so that they can then be drained and plunged into ice water to set the color. This technique, a gift of the French, is particularly effective with green vegetables such as asparagus and green beans.

BOILING OR SIMMERING MEATS AND VEGETABLES Because cooking foods in boiling or simmering water leaches them of their natural salt content, salt should be added to the water to help restore flavor.

COOKING PASTA Boiling pasta removes much of its salt content, so pasta water should be heavily salted, about 1 tablespoon for every 2 quarts of water. Measure the amount of water your pasta pot holds for each increment of pasta you will cook in it (figure on 3½ to 4 quarts water per 1 pound of pasta) and add salt as needed for the amount of water. To test whether you have used enough, taste a cooled tablespoon of the pasta water; it should be noticeably salty.

In honor of the Italians, who believe that adding salt to boiling water makes it slightly bitter (and if they don't know, who does?), add salt after the water reaches a boil rather than before. This sometimes stops the boiling for a few seconds; when the water returns to a boil, add the pasta and stir well. Time the cooking of the pasta from the moment the water resumes the boil.

CHEESE MAKING Salt is used in the making of semisoft and hard cheeses to dry out the curd so the cheese can be pressed, to flavor the cheese, to slow the growth of the starter bacteria, and to prevent spoilage. Some cheeses have salt added directly to the curd solution, some are brined, some are kneaded with salt, and some are rubbed; feta is actually pickled (that's why this cheese is so salty).

MAKING ICE CREAM Salt lowers the temperature at which water can freeze; thus salt melts ice on roads and, when combined with crushed ice packed around a container of liquid, it makes the outside of the container cold enough to freeze the contents.

AS A ROASTING BED Use rock salt as a bed to balance foods, such as oysters on the half shell, that you want to remain upright in the oven and on the table. Food roasted on a bed of salt also cooks more evenly, because the salt distributes the heat.

MAKING BREAD Salt helps to develop the gluten in bread dough, thus making a denser, more tender loaf and a golden-brown crust; this explains the loose crumb of saltless Tuscan bread. At the same time, it slows the development of the yeast, giving bread a richer flavor, besides adding its own taste.

AS A CONDIMENT Fleur de sel, the crackling-thin film of salt that forms on the surface of sea-salt pools on hot, dry days, is prized as a condiment to sprinkle on foods just before eating, both because of its crunchy texture and its bright, clean flavor. The high price of fleur de sel makes it prohibitive to use in cooking. Other specialty salts, such as those that are smoked, like Hawaiian Kai Salt, or colored with clay, like alae salt, are also used mainly as condiments, for their color as well as their flavor. Flavored salts, such as herbed salts (see below), are also used as condiments. Use any of these as a garnish or a flavor accent on food, and pass them in small bowls at the table for people to add to dishes at will.

FLAVORED SALTS Salt mixed with crushed fresh or dried herbs and spices, and/or other ingredients such as grated citrus zest, is used as both a condiment and an ingredient in foods, such as our Beef Tenderloin with Lavender Salt.

COOKING HARD- AND SOFT-BOILED EGGS A teaspoonful of salt added to the boiling water for cooking hard- and soft-boiled eggs will make the egg white coagulate and seal any cracks that develop when the eggs are added to the pan.

MAKING SAUCES BASED ON EGG YOLKS Mayonnaise and other egg-yolk-based emulsions start with a pinch of salt, because salt helps to thicken the beaten yolks.

SALT CRUSTS AND DOUGHS FOR ROASTING AND BAKING Packing meat or fish in a paste of coarse salt is an ancient way of creating a kind of salt vessel to protect the food from direct heat. As with cooking in clay, a salt crust helps food to cook evenly and keeps it moist. A dough of salt and flour does the same thing, but is a little easier to use and to remove from the food; the dough is rolled out on a pastry board, then wrapped around the food. Like salt crusts, salt doughs are not eaten.

BURYING IN SALT FOR BAKING Submerging whole fish, potatoes, and other root vegetables, or hard fruits such as winter pears, in coarse salt bakes them more evenly and seals in the moisture at the same time.

MARINATING Although it has been proven that marinating does not truly tenderize foods, it does add moisture and flavor, and salt is an indispensable ingredient in marinades.

SPICE RUBS A mixture of salt, pepper, and other spices and herbs is a fine flavor enhancer for roasted and grilled meats; unlike marinated meats, no basting is required, and a spice rub also adds more flavor than a marinade.

BRINING Brining, once a necessity for preserving meats and vegetables through the long winter months, is still used to make pickles, olives, sauerkraut, and corned beef (the "corn" refers to the coarse grains of salt used in the brine). Brining has also come back into use in the last few years as a way of adding moisture and flavor to meats and poultry. Foods such as pork chops, roast chicken, and roast turkey, which tend to dry out when cooked, gain succulence and tenderness when brined first.

ADDING TO SWEET FOODS A bit of salt added to the batter for cookies, cakes, and other baked goods brings out the flavor of the other ingredients and adds a tiny edge of its own flavor. Salt mitigates the sweetness and cuts the acidity of fruits such as pineapple and citrus. A recent trend among chefs is to sprinkle a few grains of coarse sea salt on baked goods and other desserts, for the crunchy texture and the contrast of salt and sweet.

SALT·BAKED WHOLE FISH

1 whole striped bass, rainbow trout, or other firm-fleshed white fish, 1¼ to 1½ pounds, cleaned

4 pounds rock salt

1 lemon, sliced ⅛ inch thick

1 lime, sliced ⅛ inch thick

1 clove garlic, slivered

1 small bunch fresh cilantro

Coating a fresh fish with salt and roasting it produces a very moist, naturally sweet result. Try serving this over shredded napa cabbage tossed with a little rice vinegar and pepper. Lime salt is the perfect finishing salt.

Preheat the oven to 350°F.

Rinse the fish and pat it dry; set aside. Pour half of the salt into a baking dish just big enough to hold the fish. Lay half of the lemon and lime slices on the rock salt in the center of the baking dish. Lay the fish on top of the citrus slices. Fill the fish cavity with the garlic, cilantro, 2 lime slices, and 2 lemon slices. Place the remaining lemon and lime slices on top of the fish (the fish does not need to be completely covered with them). Pour the rest of the rock salt over the fish; it should be enough to cover the fish fully (it is not necessary for the head and tail to be completely covered).

Bake the fish for 25 to 30 minutes. To test if it is done, clean away a small portion of the salt and pierce the fish with a knife; the flesh should be firm and easily pull away from the backbone.

Remove the baking dish from the oven and scoop off and discard the salt, lemons, and limes from the top of the fish. Gently peel back the skin on the fish and discard. With a fork, loosen the meat and lift it away from the bone, placing it on a warmed dinner plate. It may pull away in several pieces. Lift out the backbone and discard. Gently lift out the remaining side of fish, removing any skin still attached, and place on a second warmed plate. Serve at once.

SALT·ROASTED SALMON

2 cups kosher salt

2 salmon fillets,
7 ounces each,
with skin intact

smoked salt and
fresh lime juice
to taste

This is probably the simplest way to cook on salt, and it involves absolutely no oil. We like to finish the salmon, which comes out wonderfully moist, with a sprinkling of Hawaiian smoked kai salt and a squeeze of lime.

Pour the kosher salt into a skillet and place it over medium heat until hot, about 5 minutes. Lay the salmon fillets, skin side down, on the salt and cover the pan. Cook for 12 to 14 minutes. Remove from the heat and let the fillets sit on the hot salt in the covered pan for another 2 to 3 minutes. Uncover and test for doneness; the salmon should be opaque throughout and firm to the touch.

Carefully slip a metal spatula between the flesh and the skin of 1 fillet, lift the fillet from the skillet, and place it on a warmed dinner plate. Repeat with the second fillet. Finish each fillet with a sprinkle of smoked salt and a squeeze of lime.

SALAD WITH SALT·BRINED TROUT
AND CITRUS VINAIGRETTE

BRINE

¼ cup kosher salt

2 tablespoons sugar

2 quarts water

6 fresh sage leaves

1 clove garlic

2 whole trout, filleted
with head, tail, and
skin intact

This salad always tastes best in the fall, when the apples are crisp and just slightly tart. Brining the trout gives it a firmer texture and imparts a slightly salty, sage essence.

To make the brine, in a large pitcher, stir together the kosher salt, sugar, and water until the salt and sugar dissolve. Coarsely chop the sage and the garlic and add to the brine. Pour into a 9-by 12-inch baking dish. Place the trout fillets, skin side up, in the brine, cover, and refrigerate for 1 to 2 hours.

¼ cup fresh orange juice

2 tablespoons
rice vinegar

1 teaspoon grated
lemon zest

¼ teaspoon freshly
ground white pepper

¼ teaspoon kosher salt

2 tablespoons
extra-virgin olive oil

2 small green apples,
halved, cored, and
thinly sliced

3 celery stalks, each
about 5 inches long,
thinly sliced

3 cups mixed
salad greens

Remove the trout from the brine, rinse lightly, and pat dry. Preheat a broiler. Place the trout fillets, skin side down, on a broiler pan and broil until firm to the touch, 4 to 6 minutes. Allow the trout to cool, then separate the trout meat from the skin. Break up the meat into coarse chunks and set aside.

To make the citrus vinaigrette, in a small bowl, whisk together all the ingredients.

In a bowl, toss together the apples, celery, greens, and three-fourths of the vinaigrette. Divide the salad among 4 salad plates and top with the trout pieces, dividing evenly. Drizzle the salads with the remaining vinaigrette and serve at once.

ROASTED SAKE CRAB
WITH SALT DIPPING SAUCE

4 tablespoons
unsalted butter

2 cups sake

2 dungeness crabs,
about 1¼ pounds
each, cooked,
cleaned, and cracked

SALT
DIPPING
SAUCE

2 cloves garlic, pressed
or minced

1 teaspoon sel gris or
other coarse gray salt

½ teaspoon freshly
ground black pepper

⅓ cup fresh lemon juice

2 tablespoons finely
chopped fresh cilantro

The season for Dungeness crabs runs from November to May on the West Coast. Purchase the crabs cooked and cleaned to save time and mess. The dipping sauce has a concentrated, salty tang, so dip gingerly in the beginning.

Preheat the oven to 500°F.

In a large ovenproof sauté pan, melt the butter over medium-high heat. Add the sake, stirring to blend. Remove from the heat, add the crab pieces, and toss to coat well with the sake mixture. Place the crabs in the oven and roast, turning the crab pieces in the sake mixture once at the halfway point, for 15 minutes.

While the crabs are roasting, make the dipping sauce. In a small bowl, stir together all the ingredients and divide between 2 small dipping bowls.

Remove the crabs from the oven and divide between 2 warmed bowls. Spoon any liquid remaining in the sauté pan over the top. Sprinkle with the fresh cilantro and serve with the dipping sauce.

GRILLED SALTED CHICKEN LIVERS
AND RED ONION

1 pound chicken livers

2 tablespoons
 kosher salt

MARINADE

2 cloves garlic, crushed

¾ cup dry sherry

2 tablespoons
 extra-virgin olive oil

1 teaspoon fresh
 medium-grind
 black pepper

1 red onion, sliced
 ½ inch thick

Try these flavorful morsels over a salad of bitter greens or on grilled toasts rubbed with garlic. The salt flavors and firms the livers.

Rinse the chicken livers and drain, then trim away any fat or connective tissue. In a bowl, toss the livers with the kosher salt, then cover and refrigerate for 30 minutes. Meanwhile, make the marinade by mixing together all the ingredients in a bowl.

Remove the chicken livers from the refrigerator, rinse again with cool water, and drain. Add the chicken livers to the marinade, toss well, cover, and refrigerate for 1 to 2 hours.

Prepare a hot fire in a grill. Remove the chicken livers from the refrigerator about 10 minutes before grilling. Skewer the livers lengthwise onto four 10-inch skewers, leaving room on both ends of each skewer to permit maneuvering on the grill.

Grill the skewers, turning them several times, until the livers are firm to the touch, 8 to 10 minutes. At the same time, grill the onion slices, turning as needed, until lightly charred and slightly limp, 3 to 5 minutes. Serve the livers and onion slices warm off the grill.

SOFTENED AND MELLOWED BY THEIR
IMMERSION IN A SALT SOLUTION, PRESERVED
LEMONS AND ORANGES WILL KEEP FOR WEEKS,
READY TO ADD THEIR COLOR AND SWEET
ACIDITY TO MOROCCAN STEWS AND DESSERTS.

PRESERVED LEMONS AND ORANGES

10 to 12 meyer lemons

3 medium-sized oranges

2 cups kosher salt

2 tablespoons
coriander seed

These slightly tart, salty lemons and oranges can be used in a variety of lamb, fish, and chicken dishes and in salads. Be sure to rinse them in cool water to remove some of the brine before using, or they may be too salty.

Wash the lemons and oranges thoroughly. Pour 2 tablespoons of the kosher salt into the bottom of each of 2 quart-size canning jars with 2-part lids, or with glass lids with wire bales. Working with 1 lemon or orange at a time, stand it upright, with the stem end down, and slice it down the center, stopping within ¼ inch of the stem. Rotate the fruit a quarter turn and slice it again, so that the fruit is quartered but again stopping within ¼ inch of the stem end. Fill each fruit "flower" with 1 tablespoon of the salt. Place the lemons in one jar and oranges in the other. Add half of the remaining salt and 1 tablespoon of the coriander seed to each jar, filling the remaining space so the contents fit snugly. Seal each jar tightly with its lid.

Let the jars stand at room temperature, turning each one upside down once a day to redistribute salt. The fruit will be ready to use in 7 days. Store in the refrigerator for up to 6 months.

MOROCCAN-STYLE STEW

2 tablespoons extra-virgin olive oil, or as needed

1 cup all-purpose flour

1 teaspoon freshly ground black pepper

8 bone-in chicken thighs, skinned

1 large yellow onion, halved and sliced

1 tablespoon ground cumin

1 can (28 ounces) plum (roma) tomatoes, cut up, with juice

¼ cup chopped preserved lemon (facing page)

¼ cup chopped preserved orange (facing page)

2 cups chicken broth

½ cup green olives, pitted and chopped

A simplified adaptation of a Moroccan tagine, this fragrant stew is made particularly satisfying and interesting with the addition of preserved citrus. Serve the stew with couscous, rice, pasta, or orzo.

In a large, heavy pot, heat the 2 tablespoons olive oil over medium-high heat. Meanwhile, in a bowl, mix together the flour and pepper. Toss each chicken thigh in the flour mixture until lightly coated, shaking off the excess.

When the oil is hot, add the chicken thighs in batches and brown lightly on both sides, adding more oil if necessary. Remove each piece as it is ready and set aside on a covered plate. Add the onion to the pot and sauté over medium heat until slightly soft and translucent, about 2 minutes. Add all the remaining ingredients along with the chicken thighs and bring just to a boil. Reduce the heat to low and simmer uncovered, stirring occasionally, until the chicken is cooked through, 45 to 60 minutes. Serve warm.

The time-honored way to rescue an oversalted soup, stock, or sauce is to add a cut-up potato, which will absorb some of the salt. You can also simply add more of the other ingredients if possible, depending on the dish: more liquid, more pasta, more vegetables.

CLEANING
WITH SALT

The cleaning uses of salt are myriad, but here are some of the most basic: Keep a box of table salt in your kitchen and use it to pour on spilled beaten egg; the salt will cause the egg mixture to coagulate, making it easier to wipe up. The same holds true for burned-food spills in your oven. Any time you have a lemon shell or two in your sink, pour some salt into them and rub them on your copper pots to keep the pots shiny; a paste of egg white that has been beaten with salt and lemon juice is even better. Salt, with a little oil if necessary, is also used as a scouring material for cleaning seasoned rolled-steel pans, as soap and water will remove the seasoning oil from the metal. And when red wine is inevitably spilled on your white tablecloth, wet it with soda water and sprinkle it with salt to draw out the wine.

HARVESTING
YOUR OWN
SEA SALT

Natural salt ponds are a matter of just the right depth and extent of seawater, so that the water can evaporate, leaving salt behind. The ideal location is a sunny coast with lagoons, as is common in several sites around the Mediterranean, such as the Camargue in France, for the Mediterranean is saltier than the ocean itself. (The lack of tides in this inland sea also makes it easier to control the salt content of the ponds.) The saltworks on the Normandy coast in France and at Maldon in England may also be on the sites of natural salt ponds. And in various places on the coasts of the United States, such as Salt Point on the northern coast of California, you can harvest your own salt by simply going down to the beach and scooping up the coarse crystals that collect there between the rocks.

WHEN IT
RAINS IT
POURS

The familiar round, dark blue Morton's salt box has progressively modernized its logo over the years, but the basic image remains the same: a little girl in a rainstorm, carrying an umbrella and a round box of spilling salt.

Morton's is still the best-known iodized salt in the American heartland, far from the coasts where iodine is naturally part of the diet because it is present in the soil and in seafood. But the company made its name (and logo) by adding calcium silicate to its refined salt, thus assuring the salt would not absorb moisture from the air in wet weather and could easily be sprinkled from salt shakers. In the absence of salt treated with this additive, rice grains are sometimes added to salt shakers, as the rice absorbs some of the moisture.

THE COLORS OF SALT

Pure salt crystals are clear, but unrefined salts come in a wide range of colors, depending on their mineral content. The rock salt we buy in stores is a dull, cloudy gray, though the salt in some mines is black, red, green, blue, purple, or yellow (unrefined Indian black salt retains its natural color). When the salt is extracted by water, then boiled to evaporate the brine, the mineral content is eliminated. Some unrefined sea salts are colored by the clay in the salt ponds; this is the source of the gray in sel gris and the pale rust color of Hawaiian alae salt (though some alae salt is made by adding clay to regular sea salt). Fleur de sel is an opaque white.

SALT PLACE-NAMES

Though once they were as clear as signposts saying SALT FOUND HERE, a variety of words, prefixes, and suffixes are today like a secret code identifying the salt-laden past of towns all across Europe and the British Isles. Here are some of the most common ones:

ALES or ALS The French version of the Greek prefix *hals* (see below).

HALS A Greek prefix meaning "salt sea"; in its German form, it indicates salt towns, such as Hallstatt.

SAL The Latin word for "salt," found in such place-names as Salisbury (and in many salt-related words, such as *salutary, salubrious, salad,* and *salary*).

SALZ- "Salt" in German, as in Salzburg, near the great Austrian salt mines.

SAU- A French prefix (evolved from the Latin) meaning "salt"; the origin of the words *sauce* and *sausage*.

-WICH An English suffix that indicated a salt-producing village.

PEANUT BRITTLE
WITH COARSE SALT

ABOUT 1½ POUNDS

1½ cups sugar

1 cup water

¾ cup light corn syrup

2 cups unsalted roasted peanuts

1 tablespoon unsalted butter, plus extra for greasing

1 teaspoon vanilla extract

¾ cup coarse sea salt

This old-fashioned peanut brittle is made a little crunchier with the addition of coarse sea salt.

Butter a baking sheet. In a heavy-bottomed saucepan, combine the sugar, water, and corn syrup over medium heat. Stir until the sugar dissolves, then increase the heat to high. Boil, without stirring, until a candy thermometer registers 260°F and the syrup is light amber in color, 30 to 35 minutes. Reduce the heat to medium-low, add the peanuts and butter, and cook, stirring constantly, until the thermometer registers 295°F, about 15 minutes.

Add the vanilla, stir well, remove from the heat, and pour out onto the prepared baking sheet. Spread the mixture into a thin sheet with the back of a buttered spoon or a buttered spatula. Sprinkle evenly with the coarse salt while still warm.

Let cool, then break into serving pieces. Store between sheets of waxed paper in an airtight container at room temperature.

SALTED ALMOND TUILES

½ cup sugar

¼ cup almonds, toasted
    and finely ground

¼ cup all-purpose flour

2 egg whites

5 tablespoons unsalted
   butter, melted

¼ teaspoon almond
   extract

¼ teaspoon vanilla
   extract

½ cup chopped
   toasted almonds

2 teaspoons fleur de sel

Toasted almonds and salt make a delightful fusion, especially when enhanced with a little sweetness. One of these delicate tuiles is the perfect resting spot for a scoop of French vanilla ice cream.

Preheat the oven to 325°F. Line a baking sheet with parchment paper.

In a bowl, combine the sugar, ground almonds, flour, egg whites, butter, and almond and vanilla extracts. Stir until well blended. Drop rounded, heaping teaspoons of the batter onto the prepared baking sheet, spacing them about 4 inches apart. Sprinkle evenly with the chopped almonds.

Bake the tuiles until golden brown, about 8 minutes. Remove from the oven and immediately sprinkle with the fleur de sel, using a generous ⅛ teaspoon for each tuile. While the tuiles are warm, carefully remove them from the baking sheet with a spatula and drape them over a rolling pin or wine bottle to cool. Store in an airtight container at room temperature.

LEMON PEPPER ORANGE—BLACK PEPPER SYRUP GREEN PEPPER AND CURRY BLEND

PEPPERY BLOODY MARY ROASTED-ASPARAGUS OMELET PEPPER, GRUYÈRE, AND

GREEN ONION BISCUITS CAULIFLOWER AND PEPPER HUMMUS CHEESE AND

PEPPER CRISPS PARMESAN PEPPER RISOTTO CORN, GREEN ONION, AND GREEN

PEPPERCORN SOUFFLÉ GARLIC, GINGER, AND PEPPER SOUP SEA SCALLOPS

WITH TOMATO-PEPPER VINAIGRETTE SALAD WITH PEPPERED TUNA CROUTONS AND WASABI

DRESSING PEPPER PORK SATAY WITH PEANUT DIPPING SAUCE MUSHROOM PEPPER

SAUCE BEEF TENDERLOIN WITH LAVENDER SALT PEPPERED PRAWNS WITH FROZEN MANGO

CLAMS IN PEPPER BROTH GRAPEFRUIT AND PEPPER GRANITA FIGS IN PEPPERED PORT

CHOCOLATE AND PINK PEPPERCORN COOKIES GREEN AND BLACK PEPPER TEA

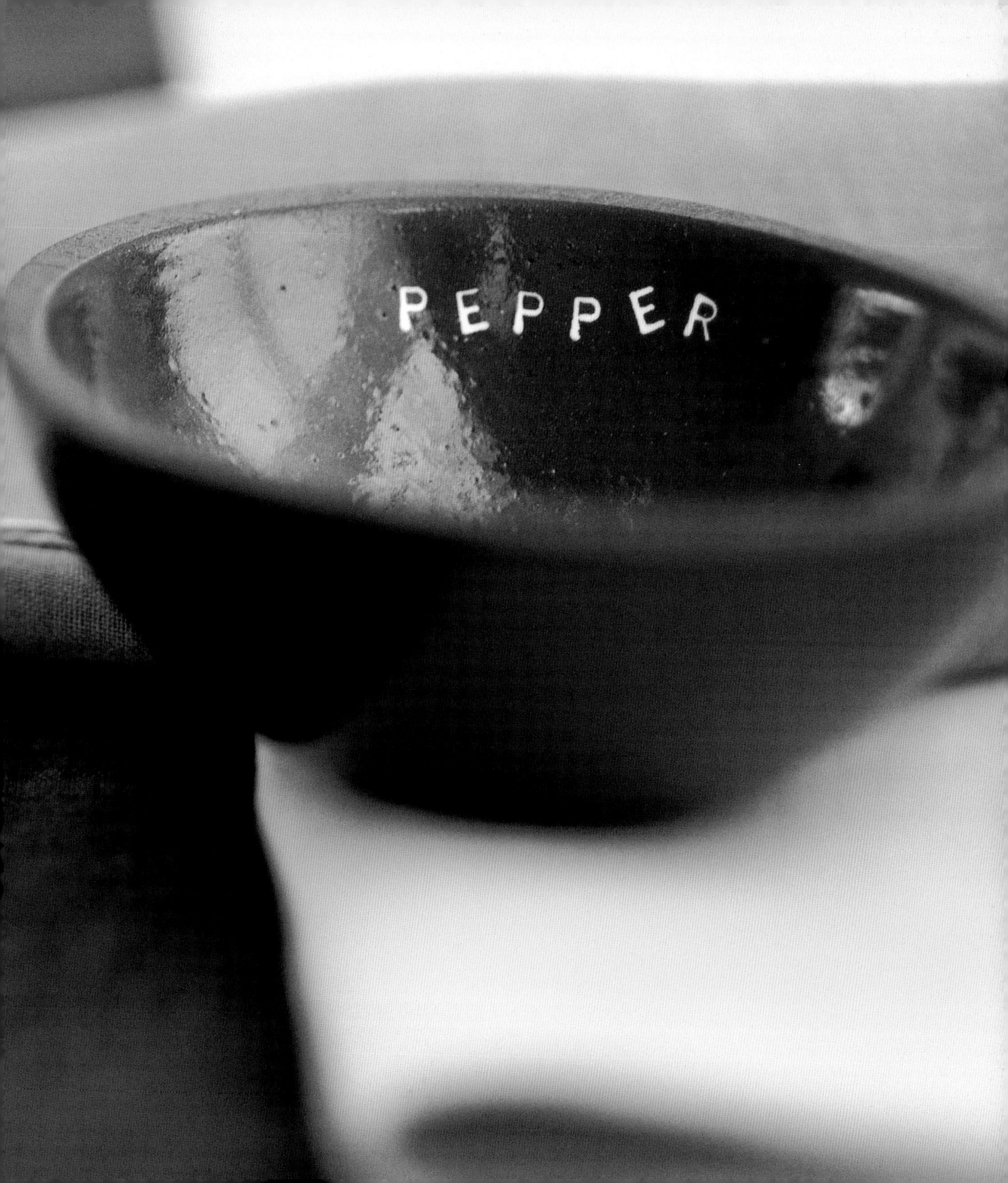
PEPPER

Pepper complements salt because it is in so many ways salt's opposite, in color, in origin, and in what it adds to food: a smoky heat and a pungent burst of fragrance. The sensation of spicy heat on the tongue has always been sought; although it is not a human need, it has always seemed to be a human want. The longing for the taste and sensation of what is known in Spanish as *picante* was satisfied for centuries in the cold climates of Europe by mustard, onions, garlic, and horseradish— all the ingredients that add a bite to food. But until the chili was discovered accidentally during the search for the source of pepper, no other ingredient provided quite the same satisfying combination of piquancy and aroma. ✦ Unlike salt, pepper is not essential for human survival, but like many of the things that make life worth living—music, books, art—pepper adds a spice to life that people have struggled for centuries to obtain. Pepper is the extra added ingredient that gives zing and pizzazz to savory foods, and though a dish may be perfectly edible without it, we have not been content to settle for that kind of sustenance. The fragrance of pepper—complex, rich, and warm—is so appealing that pepper oil is used in many perfumes, where it adds depth to the sweetness of the other ingredients. ✦ Also unlike salt, which is found in various forms all over the globe, pepper is an exotic, a tropical berry that grows only within fifteen degrees of the equator. Our taste for pepper probably began when that spice, along with the many others brought to Europe overland, was used to help preserve salted, dried, and smoked foods, and also to disguise the flavor of spoiled foods. The race among leading European powers to find a sea route to the source of those spices helped to create our modern world. ✦ In this chapter, you will find the breathtaking flavor of pepper married to assertive foods, as in Salad with Peppered Tuna Croutons with Wasabi Dressing, and mild ones, as in Corn, Green Onion, and Green Peppercorn Soufflé. And several recipes delve into the flavor explosion that results when pepper is mixed with very sweet foods, such as Roasted Figs in Peppered Port, and Orange—Black Pepper Syrup, which can be used in a multitude of ways. ✦ But finally, pepper may reach its ultimate glory when we sit down at the table with a bowl of salad or a hot dish before us and grind the fresh spice onto it at the last moment, releasing a cloud of fragrance and a sprinkling of piquancy that dresses our food and awakens our taste buds.

The story of pepper, and by extension, of all spices, is the story of thousands of years of struggle for the possession of tiny fragrant seeds, berries, seed-pods, strips of bark, and rhizomes. The spice trade began at some unknown time in prehistory, when the Arabs first imported spices from India and the East Indies. Some spices, such as cinnamon, had to be brought over thousands of miles of perilous open sea; once in Africa, they were initially transported overland by mules, then later were carried on camels by way of the Incense Route along the Arabian coast.

The Egyptians were among the most important customers of the Arab traders; their recorded use of pepper predates the pharoahs. Later, the high-living Romans outdid even the Egyptians in their love of Eastern luxuries, which included both long pepper and black pepper. For centuries, the source of spices was kept a secret by the Arabs, but the Greeks, and then the Romans, eventually broke their monopoly by learning the secret and sailing to India. The discovery of the monsoon winds around the first century A.D. cut the length of the journey to less than a year, and allowed the Romans to use prodigious amounts of spice in their foods and on their persons.

By the second century A.D., spices were also being brought overland from China on the Silk Route. The love of these aromatic goods was spread throughout Europe by the conquering Romans, so much so that when Alaric the Goth demanded a ransom for the city of Rome, the list included three thousand pounds of pepper. When Rome finally fell, the spice trade became centered instead in Constantinople.

Gradually, the Arabs began to expand their empire, until it reached its height in the eighth century A.D. Now, trade between the Muslims and Christians dwindled to nothing, for the collapse of the Roman Empire left the people of Europe with few goods to barter. Not until the Crusades began in the eleventh century was a direct route opened again to the spice-bearing Eastern lands. The Crusaders brought back both spices and an acquired taste for the highly seasoned foods they had eaten in the Middle East. The spice trade that resulted made fortunes and created dynasties in Europe; Venice, which began its rise by exploiting its salt beds, used the profits from the salt trade to enter the spice trade. Soon Venice led the Italian city states of Pisa and Genoa in jockeying for power and riches.

By the fifteenth century, a few European powers had developed powerful enough navies (which were able to stay at sea for years, thanks to salted fish) to begin the race to the spice lands. Christopher Columbus, who sailed for Spain, took a gamble and sailed a new course, only to find North America squarely in the way. In a fifteenth-century example of spin, the name *pepper* was given to the chilies he found instead; they are still called "hot peppers" and "chili peppers" today. And in one of the classic examples of fusion cuisine, chilies were eventually brought to Asia, where they were enthusiastically adopted and became an integral ingredient in cooking, though black pepper, long pepper, and fresh green peppercorns are still used as well.

The winner of the race for the spices was Portugal's Vasco da Gama, who reached India in 1498, allowing the Portuguese to control the spice trade for centuries, along with the Dutch, who arranged with the Portuguese to ship the spices on to northern Europe. War with Spain disrupted the Dutch shipping monopoly, and the Dutch next financed their own expedition to the East, where they managed to eventually wrest control of the spice trade from the Portuguese. Their monopoly was to last until the late eighteenth century, when spice-bearing trees and vines were successfully replanted and cultivated in the French tropical colonies. Today, though they will never be truly inexpensive when compared by weight to other foods, spices are found in small bottles and cans in every corner grocery.

THE VALUE
OF PEPPER

At one point during the Portuguese and Dutch monopoly of the spice trade, pepper was as valuable as gold. Like salt, it played a major role in the economic fortunes of people and nations. Pepper remains valuable today; unlike salt, which is widely found in abundant quantities that are easy to access, pepper is found only in tropical climates, and its availability is dependent on the weather and growth cycles, and on transport from distant lands. Finally, the great value of pepper is as a complement to salt, and in the unmatchable hot, black, smoky taste it adds to our food.

LEMON PEPPER

1 teaspoon freshly
cracked black pepper

1 tablespoon finely
grated lemon zest

This aromatic pepper turns up in Turkey Scallopini (page 114), but it is also a nice finishing pepper on grilled poultry and fish. Its fragrance holds well if it is not subjected to sustained heat.

Combine the black pepper and zest in a small bowl and mix well. Store in an airtight container in a pantry or cupboard and use within 2 to 3 days.

ORANGE–BLACK PEPPER SYRUP

A
B
O
U
T

1

C
U
P

⅓ cup honey

½ cup dry red wine

¼ cup balsamic vinegar

1½ teaspoons freshly
ground black pepper

1 teaspoon finely grated
orange zest

Easy to make and loaded with bold flavors, this syrup can be used in a variety of ways. We have drizzled it warm over bitter greens for a salad, spooned it over sliced pork roast for a main course, and dipped sliced peaches into it for dessert.

In a small saucepan, combine all the ingredients over medium heat. Heat for 2 to 3 minutes to blend the flavors. Serve warm or at room temperature.

GREEN PEPPER AND CURRY BLEND

A
B
O
U
T

¼

C
U
P

2 tablespoons brined
green peppercorns,
drained

1 teaspoon finely grated
orange zest

1 teaspoon curry
powder

1 tablespoon
balsamic vinegar

Try this aromatic green-and-gold blend in chicken curry, or mix it into ground lamb and shape into patties for the grill.

Combine the ingredients in a small bowl and mix well. Store in an airtight container in the refrigerator and use within 2 weeks.

The love of spices can be traced back at least as far as the early Egyptians, who used them to preserve their dead, to worship their gods, and to perfume themselves and their homes. Spices, including pepper, were the cherished extra ingredient that gave flavor and fragrance to life, whether crushed and mixed with oils or waxes to burn as incense, rubbed into the skin or hair, or added to food. Beginning with the Greeks, pepper was beloved above all other spices as an ingredient in cooking. The Romans adored pepper as well, not only for its taste, but also for its powers as a preservative and because it improves digestion.

We are the inheritors of that love of pepper, in more than one way. During the Dark Ages, when the spice trade slowed to a virtual halt, the people of Europe were forced to eat bland, unseasoned food, and they must have longed for spices in the same way that they longed for the sun through the cold northern winters. The desire for pepper was the engine that drove the Age of Exploration and created today's global cuisine, in which pepper is integral to almost every dish that sits on our table, and is a major ingredient in many of the highly spiced foods we love, from sausages and smoked meats to pepper-coated smoked fish to spice-rubbed and -coated roasted, grilled, and sautéed meats. At the same time, a coating of crushed pepper is used as a contrasting flavor for cheeses such as pepato and peppered goat cheese, so that the mild taste of the cheese and the hot taste of the pepper combine deliciously on the tongue.

The pungent heat of pepper is incomparable, but most small and medium-sized peppercorns have a sharp, strong taste, while larger ones have a fuller, more mellow flavor because they are more mature when picked. Malabar is considered one of the best of the medium-to-large black peppercorns, and Tellicherry, the largest of all, is thought of as the very best. Green peppercorns have a fresh taste that has been compared to that of asparagus, while pink peppercorns are lightly acidic. White peppercorns retain the heat of black pepper but little of its aroma, and they have a flavor reminiscent of wine. Sarawak white peppercorns are judged superior to others because they are cleaner and whiter due to being dried indoors by hot air; most peppercorns are dried on mats outdoors in the sun.

THE PEPPER
PANTRY

Every kitchen needs two kinds of pepper, white and black. But cooks can be as partial to one or the other as they are to sea salt or kosher salt; some claim that white pepper is a mere shadow of the real thing. But white pepper is preferred by many people for aesthetic reasons in foods such as white sauces, mayonnaise, and creamed dishes. Others routinely use only white pepper at the stove, and reserve black pepper for grinding at the table as a condiment. White pepper is more commonly used in European and Asian cuisines, while black pepper is more often used in American cooking. Pink and pickled (or fresh) green peppercorns are specialty peppers to add to food whole for a taste and color contrast; pink and dried green peppercorns, as well as four-pepper blends, can be ground over food at the last minute.

If possible, buy your pepper in very small amounts from a store that carries bulk foods, store it in a dark place, and grind it just before using. And look for some of the better peppers by name—Malabar, Sarawak, and especially Tellicherry—for their superior flavor.

CRACKING,
CRUSHING,
AND GRINDING
PEPPER

A few years ago, a leading food magazine tested the practice of adding whole peppercorns to stocks, broths, marinades, and brines and found that this added little or no pepper taste to the foods. But like the study that proved that marinating foods does not tenderize them, this revelation is largely ignored, because it is easier to use whole peppercorns in bouquets garnis and spice sachets than to use crushed or cracked peppercorns.

It is true, though, that pepper doesn't release its essential flavor until the hard outer shell of the berry is broken. One solution is to bruise the peppercorns by putting them in a heavy zippered plastic bag and lightly running a rolling pin over them without cracking them. For cracked pepper, use the same technique but with enough pressure to break the peppercorns open. For crushed pepper, use the rolling pin to break the peppercorns into particles, fine or coarse, depending on how you want to use them.

You can also use a mortar and heavy pestle to crush pepper; a mortar made of metal, rock, marble, or ceramic is better for this than a wooden mortar. Or, you may be able to adjust your pepper mill to grind loosely enough for crushed pepper. An even simpler method for cracking or crushing peppercorns is to put them on a cutting board and press down on them with the bottom of a heavy pan.

PEPPER MILLS

Freshly ground pepper is far superior to use on and in food than the pre-ground kind; the flavor and fragrance of ground pepper, like those of any ground spice, fade after about 20 minutes.

Two pepper mills are essential in the kitchen, one for black pepper and another for white, and it would be ideal to have two at the table as well. Most mills have a knob on the top that can be tightened or loosened to adjust the grind. Keep your kitchen pepper mills near the stove so you can grind pepper directly into your food. It's a good idea to keep pepper mills standing in small shallow bowls, so you can grind a quantity into the bowl whenever you need enough to measure in a spoon.

THE COLORS OF PEPPER

The different colors of pepper are a result of their processing at different stages of ripeness. Green peppercorns are picked at the most immature stage. Black peppercorns are picked at a riper point and turn black only when they dry. White peppercorns are riper still, but are soaked in water after drying to remove their dark coats. Pink peppercorns are not a true pepper; they come from a tree native to Brazil, but are included in four-color blends of peppercorns and used on their own for their bright pink color and their crunchy texture.

THE USES OF PEPPER

Like so many other once-rare substances (coffee, sugar, and chocolate among them), pepper was once used as a medicine; the first mention of such a use dates to the fifth century B.C. The idea has always seemed to be that if a material was hard to get, and therefore precious, it must somehow be valuable enough to affect the physical well-being of the human body. In the case of spices, however, it is true that they have a noticeable effect on bodily functions, for they raise body heat and induce sweating. Spices are also antibacterial, and an abundance of them was used both to help preserve foods and to mask the off odors of any spoilage, a virtue of great importance in the days before refrigeration.

Pepper is not only a digestive aid but also an appetite enhancer that can be used in all savory dishes as well as some sweet ones. Oil of pepper is used to add a warm flavor note to perfumes; in the same spirit of combining hot with sweet, some chefs add pepper to desserts, especially cakes, cookies, and fruit desserts. But then the Italians have been doing this for years, in their classic dessert of ripe strawberries sprinkled with aged balsamic vinegar and freshly ground black pepper.

The major use of pepper is, of course, as a prized seasoning that is used amply in some dishes for its inimitable heat and flavor, and in smaller amounts in almost every savory dish as a constant companion to salt.

PEPPERY
BLOODY MARY

4 cups tomato juice, chilled

¾ cup vodka, chilled

⅓ cup fresh lime juice

1 tablespoon prepared horseradish

2 teaspoons adobo sauce

1 teaspoon fine sea salt

1 teaspoon freshly ground black pepper

4 celery stalks

ice cubes

The smokiness in this drink comes from the addition of adobo sauce, a tomatoey sauce seasoned with vinegar, cumin, and garlic in which chipotle chilies (dried, smoked jalapeños) are traditionally packed. Look for chipotle chilies in adobo sauce in Mexican markets. Plan ahead and freeze some lime wedges and whole cherry tomatoes, then use them in place of ice cubes so your drink will not be diluted.

Combine all the ingredients except the celery and ice cubes in a frozen cocktail shaker or pitcher. Shake or stir well. Pour into 4 tall glasses filled with ice and garnish with the celery stalks. Serve at once.

ROASTED-ASPARAGUS OMELET

20 asparagus spears, about 1 pound total weight

1 tablespoon extra-virgin olive oil

1½ teaspoons freshly ground black pepper

¼ teaspoon coarse sea salt

OMELET

8 eggs

4 teaspoons freshly ground black pepper

4 tablespoons milk

8 tablespoons chopped smoked salmon

4 teaspoons unsalted butter

8 tablespoons finely cubed cream cheese

Roasting or grilling asparagus brings out its natural sweetness, making it a wonderful focal point for this peppery omelet.

Preheat the oven to 350°F.

Remove the tough portion of each asparagus spear by bending it until the end snaps off. In a wide, shallow bowl, whisk together the olive oil, black pepper, and sea salt. Toss the spears with the oil, coating evenly, then place in a single layer in a baking dish.

Roast until lightly golden on the bottom, 20 to 25 minutes. Remove from the oven and set aside.

For each omelet, in a small bowl, whisk together 2 eggs, 1 teaspoon black pepper, 1 tablespoon milk, and 2 tablespoons smoked salmon.

In a 6- to 8-inch nonstick sauté pan, melt 1 teaspoon of the butter over medium heat. Swirl the pan to coat the bottom, then pour in the egg mixture and swirl the pan again so it covers the bottom evenly. Cover and allow the mixture to cook until the eggs are nearly set, 3 to 4 minutes. Scatter 2 tablespoons of the cream cheese evenly over the surface, re-cover, and cook for another 30 seconds. With a spatula, gently lift or slide the omelet from the pan onto a serving plate. Lay 5 spears of roasted asparagus along the center of the omelet and roll it up. Repeat with the remaining ingredients to make 3 more omelets.

Serve the omelets warm or at room temperature, whole or sliced.

PEPPER, GRUYÈRE, AND GREEN ONION BISCUITS

2 cups all-purpose flour

2 teaspoons baking powder

¼ teaspoon baking soda

1 tablespoon freshly cracked black pepper

½ teaspoon kosher salt

5 tablespoons unsalted butter, cut into ¼-inch cubes

1 cup finely shredded gruyère cheese

¼ cup chopped green onion, including tender green tops

1 cup plus 2 table- spoons buttermilk

We sometimes split these savory biscuits to make small sandwiches of ham and a little mustard. They are also delicious paired with roasted meat and gravy for supper or with butter for breakfast.

Preheat the oven to 350°F.

In a bowl, stir together the flour, baking powder, baking soda, black pepper, and kosher salt until well mixed. Using a pastry blender, cut in the butter until the mixture resembles coarse meal. Add the cheese and green onion and stir and toss lightly to combine. Stir in the 1 cup buttermilk until the mixture forms a soft, slightly sticky ball.

With lightly floured hands, divide the dough into 12 equal portions. Form each portion into a rough ball and place on an ungreased baking sheet, spacing the balls about 1 inch apart. Brush the tops with the 2 table- spoons buttermilk.

Bake the biscuits until the tops are light brown, 15 to 20 minutes. Remove from the oven and serve hot or warm to accompany a meal or at room tem- perature for sandwiches.

CAULIFLOWER AND PEPPER HUMMUS

1½ cups cauliflower
florets

1 can (15½ ounces)
garbanzo beans,
rinsed and drained

2 cloves garlic, coarsely
chopped

¼ cup fresh lemon juice

1 tablespoon extra-
virgin olive oil

1½ teaspoons fresh
medium-grind
black pepper

Light-textured and full of flavor, this hummus is very easy to make, and even though it tastes rich, it is actually low in fat. Serve with pita bread or other flat bread or vegetables for dipping.

Place the cauliflower on a steamer rack over boiling water, cover, and steam until tender when pierced with a fork, 5 to 8 minutes. Remove from the pan and let cool. (Alternatively, drop the cauliflower into a pan of salted boiling water and boil until tender; the timing will be almost the same. Drain well and let cool.)

Place the cauliflower in a food processor with all the remaining ingredients. Process until smooth. Transfer to a bowl, cover, and chill well before serving.

CHEESE AND PEPPER CRISPS

¾ cup grated
(medium-fine)
parmigiano-reggiano
cheese

½ teaspoon fresh
coarsely cracked
black pepper

Try these crunchy cheese bites with a spoonful of chopped tomato and basil on top, or broken onto your favorite salad.

Preheat the oven to 350°F.

On a nonstick baking sheet, sprinkle the cheese, forming rounds about 2 inches in diameter and about ⅛ inch thick. Sprinkle each round with a little of the black pepper.

Bake the crisps until the edges just start to turn a light gold, 5 to 7 minutes. Using a flexible metal spatula, gently lift the crisps to a paper towel and let cool. Store the crisps in an airtight container.

PARMESAN PEPPER RISOTTO

2 tablespoons extra-virgin olive oil

1 yellow onion, finely chopped

4 thin slices prosciutto, finely chopped

2 cups arborio rice

2 cups chicken broth

2 cups water

½ cup dry white wine

1 cup grated parmigiano-reggiano cheese

1 tablespoon freshly cracked black pepper

additional grated cheese and freshly cracked pepper for serving

Unlike most recipes for risotto, this one won't keep you standing at the stove, stirring constantly. Despite the break with tradition, this slightly smoky, wonderfully peppery risotto turns out creamy and rich—the perfect comfort food. Pass additional pepper at the table for those who like more heat.

In a large, heavy-bottomed pot, heat the olive oil over medium heat. Add the onion and prosciutto and stir until the onion is soft, 3 to 5 minutes. Add the rice, chicken broth, and 1 cup of the water and bring to a boil, stirring occasionally. Reduce the heat and simmer, stirring occasionally, until the liquid is absorbed, another 8 to 10 minutes. Add the wine and the remaining 1 cup of water and cook, stirring constantly, for 10 minutes longer.

At this point, the rice should be plump and just tender to the bite and the liquid should be absorbed. Add the 1 cup cheese, stirring until the mixture becomes creamy. Mix in the 1 tablespoon black pepper. Transfer the risotto to a warmed serving dish and serve immediately. Pass additional cheese and pepper at the table.

GREEN PEPPERCORN SOUFFLÉ

4 tablespoons unsalted butter, plus extra for greasing

2 cloves garlic, minced

1 cup fresh corn kernels, minced

½ teaspoon kosher salt

1½ teaspoons dried green peppercorns, crushed

2 green onions, including tender green tops, finely chopped (about 3 tablespoons)

2½ tablespoons all-purpose flour

¾ cup milk

2 cups shredded medium-sharp cheddar cheese

3 eggs, separated

A little heartier than many of its namesakes, this fragrant soufflé is comfort food, French style. It may relax a little in stature before getting to the table, but it will still look and taste delicious.

Preheat the oven to 350°F. Generously butter six ½-cup ramekins, each 3½ inches in diameter.

In a small saucepan, melt 2 tablespoons of the butter over medium-low heat. Add the garlic and sauté, stirring, for 1 minute until fragrant. Add the corn and cook until it deepens in color and is translucent, about 2 minutes longer. Remove from the heat and stir in the kosher salt, green peppercorns, and green onions.

In a separate saucepan, melt the remaining 2 tablespoons butter over medium heat. Add the flour and cook, stirring constantly, for 2 minutes. Reduce the heat to low and stir in the milk. Cook, stirring constantly, until very thick, about 2 minutes. Remove from the heat and stir in the cheese and egg yolks, mixing well. Add the corn-and-onion mixture and again mix well.

In a large bowl, beat the egg whites to stiff peaks. Gently stir a small amount of the egg whites into the corn mixture to lighten it, then gently fold in the rest of the whites. Spoon the mixture into the prepared ramekins, filling to within about ¼ inch of the rims, and place the ramekins on a baking sheet.

Bake the soufflés until they have puffed and are golden brown, about 20 minutes. Serve immediately.

GARLIC, GINGER, AND PEPPER SOUP

8 cups chicken or vegetable broth

2 cloves garlic, minced

3 tablespoons peeled and freshly grated ginger

¼ cup rice vinegar

¾ cup low-sodium tamari or soy sauce

½ tablespoon freshly ground black pepper

We make this soup often. It is soothing and goes together quickly—just the kind of soup you appreciate when you are not feeling well. You can add tofu, shredded cooked chicken, or nearly any cooked vegetable you like with the balance of the broth and simmer until heated through.

Pour about ½ cup of the broth into a saucepan. Add the garlic, place over medium heat, bring to a gentle simmer, and cook until the garlic is soft and tender, about 3 minutes. Add the remaining broth and all the remaining ingredients and bring almost to a boil, then reduce the heat and simmer briefly to blend the flavors. Ladle into warmed bowls to serve.

SEA SCALLOPS
WITH TOMATO-PEPPER VINAIGRETTE

½ pound large sea scallops

4 cups water

TOMATO-PEPPER VINAIGRETTE

1 small to medium vine-ripened tomato, coarsely chopped

1 small clove garlic, coarsely chopped

2 tablespoons extra-virgin olive oil

1½ tablespoons rice vinegar

Robust and versatile, this pepper-laced vinaigrette is excellent on a simple scallop salad, or it can easily stand alone as a dipping sauce with bread. A ripe, sweet tomato is essential to the flavor balance of the dish.

Rinse the sea scallops and pat dry; set aside. Bring the water to a boil in a saucepan.

While the water is heating, make the vinaigrette: combine the tomato, garlic, olive oil, vinegar, black pepper, and basil in a small food processor or a blender and processing until smooth. Add sea salt to taste. The vinaigrette will be roughly the consistency of ketchup or a bit looser; set aside.

When the water comes to a boil, reduce the heat to medium. Place the scallops in the water and poach until white and firm, 2 to 2½ minutes. Pour

2 teaspoons freshly
  ground black pepper

2 fresh basil leaves,
  stemmed

  fine sea salt to taste

6 ounces mixed
  salad greens

the scallops into a colander and rinse with cool water; set aside to drain.

Divide the greens between 2 chilled salad plates. Slice each scallop in half horizontally; they should be slightly rare inside. Place the halved scallops on the greens, dividing them evenly, and drizzle with the vinaigrette. Serve immediately.

SALAD WITH PEPPERED TUNA CROUTONS

AND WASABI DRESSING

WASABI
DRESSING

1 teaspoon wasabi
  powder

3 tablespoons
  rice vinegar

3 tablespoons
  low-sodium tamari

PEPPERED TUNA
CROUTONS

¾ pound high-grade
  tuna steak, about
  1 inch thick

½ cup plain fine dried
  bread crumbs

2 tablespoons freshly
  ground black pepper

2 tablespoons
  vegetable oil

1 pound mixed
  salad greens

Here are some spicy little bites to turn your usual green salad into a light main course. For an appetizer, serve the "croutons" with the dressing for dipping, accompanied with iced sake in frozen martini glasses.

To make the dressing, whisk together all the ingredients until well blended; set aside.

To make the croutons, cut the tuna into 1-inch cubes, discarding the bone. (You should have about 20 cubes; some may be a bit irregular in shape.) In a small bowl, stir together the bread crumbs and black pepper. Working in batches, roll the tuna cubes in the bread-crumb mixture, pressing lightly to be sure the mixture adheres. Set the coated tuna aside.

In a skillet, heat the vegetable oil over high heat. When the oil is very hot but not smoking, gently drop the tuna into the skillet and reduce the heat to medium. Spread the cubes evenly in the pan, then immediately begin to turn each cube over with tongs. By the time you turn each one over, they should all be done, about 4 minutes total cooking time. They should be lightly golden to medium brown and slightly rare in the center. Remove from the pan and keep warm.

Place the salad greens in a bowl and toss with the dressing. Divide evenly among 4 salad plates and top with the warm tuna croutons. Serve at once.

PEPPER PORK SATAY

WITH PEANUT DIPPING SAUCE

1 pork tenderloin,
  1 to 1¼ pounds

MARINADE

½ cup light soy sauce

1 tablespoon peeled
  and minced fresh
  ginger

2 tablespoons fresh
  medium-grind
  black pepper

1 tablespoon dried
  green peppercorns,
  crushed

¼ cup rice vinegar

2 tablespoons
  vegetable oil

PEANUT
DIPPING
SAUCE

¼ cup creamy
  peanut butter

¼ cup water

2 teaspoons peeled and
  minced fresh ginger

1 tablespoon
  low-sodium soy sauce

1 tablespoon
  rice vinegar

1 tablespoon chopped
  fresh cilantro

Serve this Southeast Asian–inspired appetizer hot and peppery right off the grill, or cook the skewers up to 1 hour in advance and wrap them in foil until serving. You can also grill the meat without the skewers; the cooking time is the same. Serve with rice noodles.

Slice the pork tenderloin in half crosswise, then cut each half lengthwise into ½-inch-wide strips. (You should have 8 to 10 strips.) Whisk together all the ingredients for the marinade in a baking dish. Add the pork strips and turn to coat evenly. Cover and marinate for up to 1 hour in the refrigerator. Remove from the refrigerator 5 to 7 minutes before grilling.

Soak 8 to 10 wooden skewers, each 8 inches long, in water to cover for at least 20 minutes. Prepare a hot fire in a grill.

Meanwhile, prepare the dipping sauce: In a small bowl, stir together all the ingredients. Divide among 4 small dipping bowls.

Drain the skewers, then weave a pork strip onto each skewer. Place the skewers over the fire and grill, turning once, about 3 minutes on each side. The pork is done when it is firm to the touch. Serve with the peanut dipping sauce.

MUSHROOM PEPPER SAUCE

A RICHLY FLAVORED AND
QUICKLY MADE SAUCE OF FRESH
MUSHROOMS, RED WINE, DRIED
PLUMS, AND CRACKED PEPPER
ADDS A DEEP FLAVOR NOTE AND
AUTUMNAL COLOR TO A VARIETY
OF DISHES, SUCH AS PASTA,
MASHED POTATOES, ROAST PORK,
AND ROAST CHICKEN.

MUSHROOM PEPPER SAUCE

1 tablespoon extra-virgin olive oil

1 shallot, chopped

⅓ cup dried plums (prunes), pitted and chopped

½ pound assorted fresh mushrooms, brushed clean and chopped

1 cup medium-dry red wine

1 teaspoon balsamic vinegar

½ teaspoon kosher salt

½ teaspoon freshly cracked black pepper

This warming, rich sauce quickly lends depth to any chosen dish, from pork roast to roast chicken to mashed potatoes. When the sauce is finished, taste to adjust the level of pepper as desired, increasing it in increments of ¼ teaspoon at a time.

In a saucepan, heat the olive oil over medium heat. Add the shallot and sauté until it begins to turn golden, about 2 minutes. Add the dried plums and mushrooms and sauté, stirring several times, until the mushrooms are soft and browned, 1 to 2 minutes. Add the wine, vinegar, kosher salt, and black pepper and cook, stirring, until the flavors are melded, 2 to 3 minutes longer. Serve warm.

BEEF TENDERLOIN
WITH LAVENDER SALT

1 whole beef tenderloin,
5 to 6 pounds,
trimmed of excess
fat and silver skin

2 tablespoons lavender
salt (page 16)

2 tablespoons freshly
cracked black pepper

2 tablespoons
extra-virgin olive oil

If you like beef, this is one of the easiest and most impressive dishes you can make and serve.

Remove the beef from the refrigerator 1 hour before roasting. Preheat the oven to 425°F.

Just before the beef goes in the oven, rub it with the lavender salt, the black pepper, and the olive oil. Set a rack in a shallow roasting pan and set the beef on the rack. Place in the oven and roast until an instant-read thermometer inserted into the thickest part of the roast registers 125°F. The meat will be rare to medium-rare.

Transfer the meat to a warmed platter, tent with aluminum foil, and allow to stand for 30 minutes before carving.

PEPPERED PRAWNS
WITH FROZEN MANGO

3 large, ripe mangoes

20 large prawns

1½ teaspoons freshly
ground dried green
peppercorns

1½ teaspoons szechuan
peppercorns, crushed

1½ teaspoons
ground cumin

1 teaspoon kosher salt

¼ cup sugar

2 tablespoons water

Frozen, sweet mango provides a pleasant, cool contrast that complements these spicy prawn appetizers. Szechuan peppercorns, which are light to medium brown and split and flowerlike in appearance, can be found in Asian markets or specialty foods stores.

Working with 1 mango at a time, stand the mango lengthwise and cut from top to bottom on one flat side as close to the pit as possible. Repeat on the opposite side. You should end up with 2 halves. Discard the pit. With a spoon, scrape the pulp from the skin into a bowl. Repeat with the remaining 2 mangoes. Mash the pulp with a fork until smooth, then cover and freeze for at least 30 minutes. (If you leave it for over 1 hour, be sure to mash it again, so it is not frozen solid when you are ready to serve it.)

Peel each prawn, leaving the tail segment intact. Devein, rinse, and pat dry. In a small bowl, combine the green peppercorns, Szechuan peppercorns, cumin, and kosher salt; set aside. Line a baking sheet with parchment paper.

In a saucepan, heat the sugar and water over medium-high heat. Stir until the sugar dissolves, then continue to heat until the mixture bubbles and just begins to turn golden. Carefully place half the prawns in the pan. Turn them over after 1 minute, and continue to cook until they are pink and cooked through, about 1 minute longer. Remove them to the parchment-lined baking sheet. Cook the remaining prawns in the same way. Sprinkle the warm prawns with the pepper mixture, coating on both sides.

Serve the prawns warm or at room temperature with the frozen mango alongside.

CLAMS IN PEPPER BROTH

2 tablespoons extra-virgin olive oil

2 cloves garlic, minced

2 pounds clams, scrubbed

1 cup dry white wine

2 tablespoons unsalted butter

1 teaspoon freshly ground black pepper

2 tablespoons chopped fresh flat-leaf (italian) parsley

¼ teaspoon finely grated lemon zest

Light, yet full of bright flavors, these clams are a wonderful appetizer, served with good, crusty bread. You can also serve them over pasta.

In a large sauté pan, heat the olive oil over medium heat. When the oil is hot, add the garlic and sauté for about 30 seconds until fragrant. Add the clams and stir until the clams begin to open, about 3 minutes. Add ½ cup of the wine and continue to stir, removing any opened clams from the pan and placing them in a bowl. Continue to stir just until all the remaining clams are opened, 4 to 6 minutes' total cooking time. Transfer the clams to the bowl, discarding any that did not open.

With the pan over medium heat, add the remaining ½ cup wine, the butter, and the black pepper. Stir until the butter is melted. Return the clams to the pan, including any juices in the bowl, and stir the clams in the broth for another 2 minutes to blend the flavors. Add the parsley and lemon zest, mix well, and immediately remove from the heat.

Spoon the clams into 2 warmed bowls, dividing evenly. Spoon any broth remaining in the pan over the clams. Serve at once.

GRAPEFRUIT AND PEPPER GRANITA

2 cups fresh
    grapefruit juice

2 tablespoons sugar

½ teaspoon fresh
    fine- to medium-grind
    black pepper

We sometimes serve this on summer evenings after a meal cooked on the grill. It is cleansing and light, just a little sweet, and warming.

In a bowl that can be put into the freezer, stir together the grapefruit juice and sugar until the sugar dissolves, then stir in the black pepper. Place the bowl in the freezer until the mixture is frozen, about 1 hour. Remove from the freezer and break the mixture up with a fork until no chunks remain. Return the bowl to the freezer and freeze for 30 minutes longer. At the same time, place 4 stemmed glasses in the freezer.

Remove the granita from the freezer and again break it up with a fork until no chunks remain. Spoon into the frozen stemmed glasses and serve immediately.

FIGS IN PEPPERED PORT

1 cup port

½ tablespoon freshly
    cracked black pepper

4 medium-to-large figs,
    halved lengthwise

1 pint vanilla ice cream
    (optional)

Soothing and sweet, this is the perfect dessert for a chilly fall evening.

In a saucepan, combine the port and black pepper and bring to a simmer over medium heat. Carefully place the fig halves in the liquid and simmer for 2 to 3 minutes to soften slightly. With a slotted spoon, remove the figs to a bowl. Continue to simmer the wine mixture for 2 minutes to reduce slightly. Pour the sauce over the figs.

To serve, divide the fig halves and the sauce evenly among 4 warmed dessert bowls, or place a scoop of vanilla ice cream in each of 4 bowls and spoon the fig halves and sauce over the top. Serve at once.

CHOCOLATE AND PINK PEPPERCORN COOKIES

¾ cup all-purpose flour

½ teaspoon
  baking powder

¼ teaspoon kosher salt

½ cup (1 stick) unsalted
  butter, at room
  temperature

⅔ cup firmly packed
  brown sugar

⅓ cup unsweetened
  cocoa powder

1½ teaspoons
  vanilla extract

2 egg whites

4 tablespoons
  freshly crushed pink
  peppercorns

FILLING

1 cup mascarpone
  cheese

¼ cup confectioners'
  sugar

Here is a rich little chocolate cookie with an unexpected crunch and a floral undertone from the addition of pink peppercorns. The subtle fragrance of the peppercorns mates particularly well with chocolate.

Preheat the oven to 325°F. Line 2 baking sheets with parchment paper.

In a small bowl, stir together the flour, baking powder, and salt until well mixed. In a medium bowl, using an electric mixer or a wooden spoon, cream together the butter and brown sugar until light and creamy. Beat in the cocoa and vanilla. Add the egg whites one at a time, beating well after each addition. Stir in the flour mixture.

Drop the cookie dough by teaspoons onto the prepared baking sheets, spacing the cookies about 2 inches apart. Sprinkle each mound with about ¼ teaspoon of the crushed pink peppercorns.

Bake the cookies until firm and dry to the touch, 10 to 12 minutes. Remove from the oven and cool on a rack.

While the cookies are cooling, make the filling: In a bowl, stir together the cheese and confectioners' sugar until well blended.

When the cookies are cool, spoon a heaping teaspoon of the filling on the flat side of half of the cookies, spreading it to within about ¼ inch of the edge. Top with a second cookie, pressing the flat side against the filling. Store in an airtight container in the refrigerator.

GREEN AND BLACK PEPPER TEA

½ teaspoon dried green peppercorns, crushed

½ teaspoon black peppercorns, crushed

1 slice fresh ginger

½ teaspoon dried mint

2 cups boiling water

sugar or honey

Black pepper is believed to aid digestion, improve circulation, and ease stiffness and pain. Try some of this curative blend, and see what you think.

Combine the green and black peppercorns, ginger, and mint in a tea ball, and place in a teapot. Pour in the boiling water and let steep for 3 minutes. When the tea is ready, pour into 2 cups and add sugar or honey to taste.

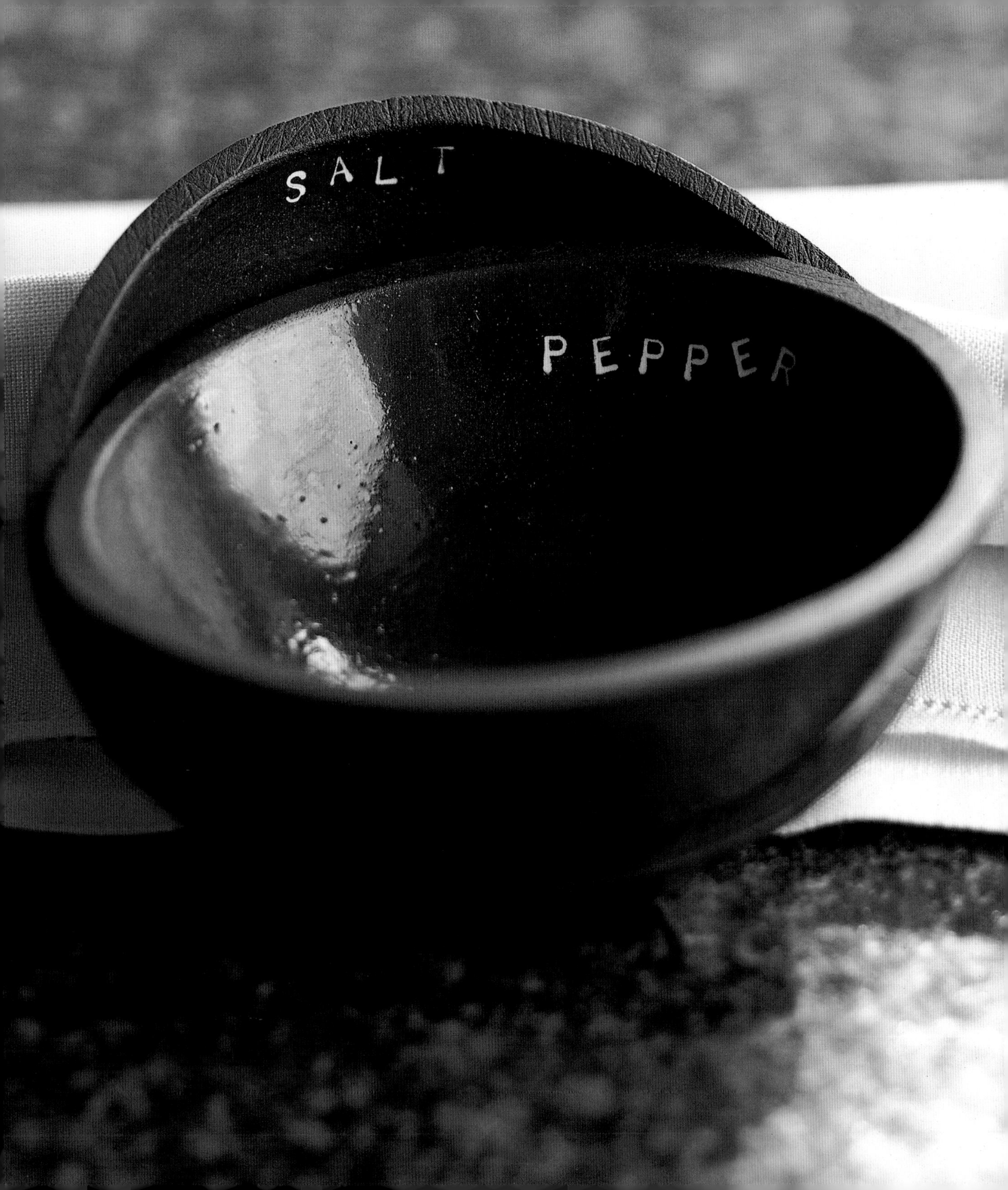
SALT
PEPPER

CUMIN, SALT, AND PEPPER SALT AND PEPPER ROASTED GARLIC PASTE SALT AND

PEPPER MARTINI ONIONS SALT AND PEPPER CANDIED PECANS PICKLED BEANS AND LEEKS

GRAVLAX-STYLE HALIBUT ROASTED GARNET SWEET POTATOES SPOON BREAD ROASTED

TOMATO SOUP SALT AND PEPPER FOCACCIA GRILLED PORTOBELLO MUSHROOM PANINI

SALT AND PEPPER CARBONARA CHICKEN-APPLE SAUSAGES WITH SAUTÉED GRAPES

TURKEY SCALLOPINI TURKEY JERKY PEPPERED POT ROAST SALT AND PEPPER FRIED

SAGE LEAVES THREE-PEPPER-BRINED ROAST CHICKEN SALT-ROASTED PEARS

WITH CAMEMBERT SALTED TANGERINE SECTIONS WITH PEPPER DIPPING SAUCE

Like partners in a good marriage, salt and pepper bring out the best in each other; in fact, they need each other for balance and completion. White and black, savor and heat, mineral and vegetable, they are opposites that together are more than the sum of their parts. ✦ Almost any savory dish—and a few sweet ones—that uses salt calls out for pepper as well, even some whose main piquancy derives from chilies. A dish without the added kick of pepper's heat seems boring, like a pale imitation of itself. With dishes that use goodly amounts of both salt and pepper like the ones in this chapter, the trick is to achieve the right balance, so that neither seasoning overwhelms the other or the other ingredients in the dish. ✦ Some dishes depend on a robust use of this pair for their exuberance, such as salt and pepper shrimp; or spice cakes, cookies, and breads with just the right amount of heat and savor (a little black pepper gives them the faintest dark edge that makes them much more interesting without being identifiable); or peppered steak, in which the rich flavor of beef is balanced with a warming crust of salt and pepper; or any food that uses a marinade or spice rub to give it a haunting or exhilarating depth of flavor. Lamb, tuna, duck, and venison are other assertive-tasting foods that profit from the dynamic interaction of salt and pepper, and both turkey and pork will be juicier and better flavored when they have been brined in a solution that contains pepper and other spices. ✦ Salt-and-pepper mixtures, kept on hand in the kitchen or made up at the last minute before adding to a dish, are one of the most obvious ways to add the sparkle and fire of salt and pepper to food. And because both salt and pepper are appetite enhancers, appetizers, first courses, hors d'oeuvres, and garnishes that use robust amounts of them are some of the best uses of these seasonings. ✦ This chapter contains a cluster of these kinds of recipes, including Salt and Pepper Fried Sage Leaves to crush and sprinkle over soup or pasta or to use as a garnish; Salt and Pepper Candied Pecans to add to salads or to serve as an appetizer; and first courses such as Roasted Tomato Soup and Salt and Pepper Focaccia. There are main courses as well, such as Three-Pepper-Brined Roast Chicken and Peppered Pot Roast. Combining any of these highly spiced dishes with milder foods will add balance and excitement to your table. And the individual glossaries in this chapter will help you to identify the specific salts and peppers used in our recipes.

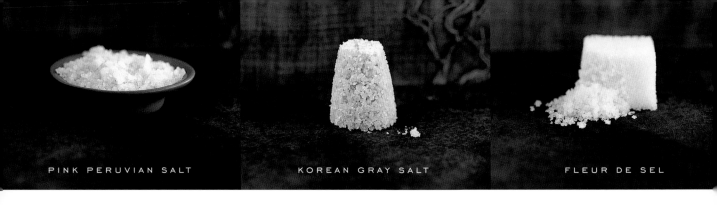

PINK PERUVIAN SALT   KOREAN GRAY SALT   FLEUR DE SEL

SALT
GLOSSARY

ARTISAN SALTS Hand-gathered sea salts, which include fleur de sel and sel gris.

BAY SALT Another term for sea salt; the name is now generic, though it originally referred to a cheap, impure salt from Bourgneuf Bay on the French coast.

BLOCK SALT Rock salt that has been made into a brine, evaporated, and poured while hot into molds. It is rarely produced now, but in the past, this salt, which must be scraped from the block, was used in making brines and pickles.

CONDIMENT SALTS Salts that are used only as a garnish just before serving or eating, not in cooking, because of their special flavor and texture. Also known as finishing salts, they include fleur de sel, salts that are colored with clay or lava, and blends of sea salt and herbs or other flavorings.

INDIAN BLACK SALT A brownish-black rock salt, available in Indian markets in chunks or ground, which turns it a pinkish brown. It has a strong sulfuric taste and fragrance, but adds very little actual saltiness to food. Use sparingly as a condiment or garnish for its color.

IODIZED SALT In the 1920s, iodine began to be added to salt when it was learned that lack of iodine in the diet was the cause of goiters in people living in some landlocked areas such as the American Midwest and Switzerland. People who live near the ocean ingest sufficient iodine from eating seafood, drinking the local water, and eating locally grown vegetables and fruits that absorb iodine from the soil. Most table salt and some refined sea salts have been iodized, which adds a slight aftertaste.

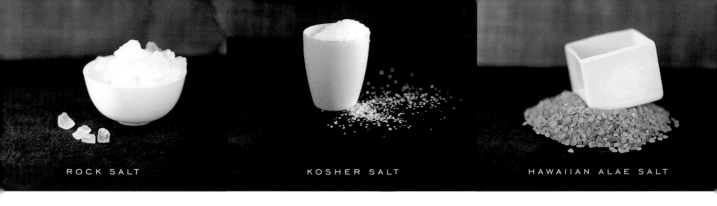

ROCK SALT KOSHER SALT HAWAIIAN ALAE SALT

KOSHER SALT Large salt crystals, shaped like hollow pyramids, used in koshering meats because the crystals stay on the surface of the meat and so help to draw out the blood. (According to Jewish dietary laws, kosher meats must have as much of the blood removed as possible.) Kosher salt is beloved in cooking, especially by many American chefs, because it is easy to pick up in the fingers, it has no additives, and it is both inexpensive and of high quality.

PICKLING SALT A finely ground salt with no additives, used to pickle foods commercially because it dissolves quickly and won't cloud the brining solution.

PINK PERUVIAN SALT Also called Andean salt, this beautiful pale pink salt is harvested high in the Andes, two hundred miles inland, from terraced salt beds. The source is an ancient dried sea with a red clay bed, rich with trace minerals. The salt is cut into blocks, then carried on llamas for hundreds of miles to the nearest town to be ground into coarse crystals. Sprinkle it on sliced vine-ripened tomatoes at the table.

ROCK SALT Salt from underground deposits; relatively unrefined, its grayish hue reflects its natural mineral content. For millennia, rock salt was mined with picks and chisels, but today it is extracted by being dissolved in water from high-pressure hoses. The resulting brine is then pumped out and evaporated to produce the coarse crystals we use to freeze ice cream and to melt ice on roads.

SEA SALT Salt retrieved from the living body of the sea, usually in salt farms along the shore. The first sea salt was probably gathered from shallow lagoons, but soon people learned to make salt beds wherever a clay-rich soil allowed them to. It was the Romans who first farmed salt by

constructing a series of salt beds at gradually declining levels (and increasing salinity) and by controlling the flow of seawater into the beds.

Sea salts may be completely unrefined—the result of solar evaporation in the same kind of shallow ponds created by the Romans—or refined, the product of evaporation by boiling sea water in huge vats. Sea salt is available either naturally coarse or ground into fine grains. The crystals take various shapes, from jagged, hollow pyramids to shards and flakes. Unless you need added iodine in your diet, look for sea salt that has not been iodized (see Iodized Salt).

Sea salt is prized for its mineral content, which can color it and also give it a more complex, faintly sweet taste; sea salt also retains some of the flavor of the sea. Salts from different areas may have subtly different tastes, and some dissolve more quickly than others, depending on the size and form of the crystals. Some sea salt is so moist that it is hard to measure accurately, but it is good to add to pasta water and the water for cooking vegetables, and is perfect for making herb blends and for packing into crusts for roasting fish and meat. Use fine-grained sea salt for making vinaigrettes and sauces, and in salt shakers at the table, as it dissolves more quickly than coarse sea salt. Dry coarse sea salt can be used in salt grinders.

There are many other sources for sea salts besides the ones mentioned here, including Tunisia and Mallorca. The salts that follow are some of the most popular sea salts available now.

Camargue Salt A coarse salt from some of the oldest salt gardens in the world, the vast salt lagoons between Arles and Aigues-Mortes in southwest France. The sea here is ten times as salty as the open ocean. Much Camargue salt is industrially produced, but salt is still gathered here by hand, and fleur de sel is harvested as well.

Celtic Gray Sea Salt See Sel Gris.

Danish Smoked Salt A dark brown coarse salt that is smoked over wood and used as a condiment.

Fleur de Sel The "flower of the salt" is the crackling-thin layer of crystallized salt that "blooms" on the top of salt ponds on sunny, windy afternoons.

It is gathered by hand in northwestern France, Portugal, and the Camargue in the south of France. The most expensive form of salt, it is used as a condiment to sprinkle on food just before eating, for its texture and flavor. Because it rises to the top of the ponds, it leaves behind much of the clay that colors the salt below it, so it is an opaque white rather than gray, and the complex flavor of its lacy flakes is minerally, with a hint of sweetness.

Gros Sel The French term for coarse sea salt.

Halen Môn The brand name of a delicately flavored salt now being produced near Anglesey, Wales.

Hawaiian Alae Salt Sea salt from Hawaii, either naturally colored by iron oxide in the red clay of the salt ponds, or by clay being added to the salt. Used ritually in Hawaii for centuries, and as an ingredient in some fish dishes (such as *poke*), it is prized as a condiment because of its pale rusty color. Use with mild-flavored foods, especially fish. Also spelled *alaea* or *ala'e*.

Hawaiian Black Lava Salt A coarse condiment salt from Hawaii, colored by the addition of finely ground black lava and activated charcoal. Its faintly earthy taste is good with assertive-tasting fish like salmon, and it makes a dramatic garnish.

Hawaiian Smoked Kai Salt A light brown coarse salt smoked over kai wood; it has a slightly smoky taste and is used as a condiment. Try it on deviled eggs, or on grilled fish, meat, or chicken.

Korean Gray Salt A coarse salt available in some Asian markets. It can be substituted for sel gris in most recipes.

Maldon Salt A soft salt with a delicate taste and hollow, pyramid-shaped crystals, from Maldon, Essex, on the English coast. Use to garnish mild-flavored dishes.

Oshima Island Salt Small, flaky crystals of Japanese sea salt from an island near Tokyo; marketed as Oshima Island Red Label salt.

Portuguese Salt Sea salt from salt pans off the Algarve, on the southern coast of Portugal. Salt is also produced inland from a salt spring in the village of Rio Maior.

Sel Gris Moist, coarse sea salt from the Atlantic Coast of France, colored gray from the clay of the salt pans. Also called Celtic gray sea salt, it is produced in Guérande, on the Breton Ile de Ré (from salt gardens built by Cistersian monks in the fourteenth century); on the Breton island of Noirmoutier, where salt was also first harvested by monks; and on the Brittany and Normandy coasts.

Sicilian Salt A generic name for sea salts from Sicily; includes Trapani salt, below.

Trapani Salt Considered by some chefs to be the best-tasting of all sea salts, Trapani salt is produced near a city of the same name in Sicily. The pumps that bring the water to the ponds are powered by windmills, and the large crystals are ground by stone wheels to make hard, dry grains.

SEASONED SALT Lawry's seasoned salt (made with added garlic powder, paprika, and other seasonings) and lemon-pepper salt have been available in supermarkets for years. Some cooks like to make their own special combinations of herbs, spices, and salt to keep on hand in the kitchen. Seasoned gray sea salts and fleurs de sel from Europe may be found in some specialty foods stores and online; these coarse salts are combined with crushed dried herbs such as rosemary and thyme, to add not only flavor, but also texture and visual beauty when sprinkled on salads and other foods at the table.

SOUR SALT Not really salt, but citric acid derived from acidic fruits such as citrus. It looks like regular salt, and is used by people on salt-restricted diets, as well as in the food industry.

TABLE SALT Highly refined rock or sea salt, which may or may not have iodine added. Because the salt has been refined, it contains no minerals and so takes the shape of a pure salt crystal: a tiny, exact square. It also has a sharper and somewhat bitter taste compared to sea salt (see Iodized Salt).

The three kinds of true peppercorns—black, green, and white—are berries picked from the same tropical vine, *Piper nigrum*, at different stages of ripeness. Native to the forests of Travancore and Malabar, on the Indian coast, pepper is now grown in tropical climates in countries around the world, including Indonesia, Malaysia, Brazil, China, Vietnam, Micronesia, Madagascar, Thailand, and Nigeria.

BLACK PEPPER Picked just before the berries begin to redden, black peppercorns are dried in the sun, which makes their skin turn dark. Quality is judged by size, for the ripest berries are also the largest and most flavorful.

Lampong Black peppercorns from the Indonesian island of Sumatra.

Malabar Large black peppercorns from Malabar, on the west coast of southern India, considered to have the best flavor among the mass-produced peppers.

Mangalore Black peppercorns from the Malabar coast of India.

Sarawak Fairly large black peppercorns from the Malaysian island of Sarawak. Also available white.

Tellicherry More mature, and thus large, black peppercorns from the northern Malabar coast of India, prized for their fully developed, rich flavor.

CLUSTER PEPPER Clusters of green peppercorns may be available in some Asian markets in the United States, but are more common in Australia and Southeast Asia. They are nice to use as a garnish, or the berries can be crushed and added to food for their bright color and mildly peppery flavor.

GREEN PEPPER Unripened pepper berries, picked while green and soft. Available in the United States preserved in brine or vinegar, or dried. Their color is a drawing card in some dishes, as is the tender texture of the bottled peppercorns. Their flavor is mild and slightly grassy. Pickled green peppercorns are a nice contrast when added to rich sauces and pâtés; be sure to rinse them before using. The flavor of the ground dried peppercorns fades quickly, so green pepper should be ground and added to food just before serving or at the table. Fresh green peppercorns are available in summer and winter in Asia and Australia; used in Thai food and other Southeast Asian cuisines, they are crushed and added to curry pastes, soups, and sauces (see Cluster Pepper).

LONG PEPPER This spice, with its inch-long rod-shaped berries, is not a true pepper, though it is a relative of *Piper nigrum*. Always used whole, long pepper is milder than black pepper, though its taste is very similar. It grows wild in a swatch stretching from southern India to the foothills of the Himalayas. Perhaps because it may have been the first pepper imported into the Mediterranean, long pepper was particularly prized by the Romans. Today, it is used mostly in Asian cuisines, especially in pickling and brining.

PINK PEPPER The bright pink berries of a South American tree, pink peppercorns are peppercorns in name only. They are one of the colors in four-color blends of peppercorns, and are just the right touch in some mild dishes. Especially nice with fish or in cream sauces, they add a spark of color, a pleasant crunch, and a delicate, lightly acidic flavor. If ground, they should be added to food at the last minute, as their flavor quickly wanes.

SZECHUAN PEPPER Like the pink peppercorn, Szechuan pepper berries are the same shape and size as true peppercorns, but they come from the prickly ash tree, not the pepper vine. They are supposedly native to the Chinese province after which they are named. The berries are used in Szechuan cuisine, as well as in the cuisine of Xinjiang, China's disputed western province. They have a completely different taste and aroma from true pepper—they are milder, and have a spicy hint of clove and ginger, though they also have a numbing effect on the tongue when eaten whole. Available whole or ground; whole berries should be heated before being ground.

WHITE PEPPER Almost-ripe peppercorns, whose skin is loosened in water and removed before the berries are dried. Less aromatic than black pepper, but with a hot, winelike flavor, white pepper is preferred for use in light-colored foods and is popular in Southeast Asian and European cuisines.

Muntok White peppercorns from the Indonesian island of Bangka, these are processed by being soaked in water until their outer coating loosens.

White Sarawak White peppercorns from Malaysia, which are processed in the running streams. They are air-dried rapidly indoors with hot air, unlike most peppercorns, which are dried in the sun. As a result, they are cleaner, whiter, and have a clearer taste than other white peppercorns.

CUMIN, SALT, AND PEPPER

¼ CUP

1 tablespoon freshly ground black pepper

2 tablespoons cumin seed, toasted in a dry pan until fragrant and then crushed

1 tablespoon coarse sea salt

This aromatic blend is all you need to season a pot roast. It also works well as a rub on meats for grilling, such as flank steak for fajitas.

Combine the ingredients in a small bowl and mix well. Store in an airtight container in a cupboard or pantry and use within 4 to 6 weeks.

SALT AND PEPPER ROASTED GARLIC PASTE

ABOUT ¾ CUP

4 whole heads garlic

½ cup extra-virgin olive oil

1 teaspoon coarse sea salt

1 teaspoon freshly ground black pepper

The flavor of roasted garlic spread is full, yet not overwhelming like fresh garlic. The texture is smooth and can easily replace mayonnaise in many instances. Garlic spread will keep up to one week in a tightly sealed container in the refrigerator.

Preheat the oven to 375°F. Peel away the loose, outer, papery layers from the garlic heads. Trim off the pointy end of each head to expose the tops of the cloves. (Cutting off about ½ inch will generally do it.) Place the garlic heads, cut sides up, in a small baking dish or individual soufflé cups. Drizzle them with the olive oil and sprinkle with the coarse salt and black pepper.

Roast the garlic heads until the cloves are golden brown and begin to push out of the bulb, about 45 minutes. Remove from the oven, let cool, then squeeze the roasted garlic cloves out of heads into a small bowl. Mash with a fork, pour the oil from the baking dish into the mashed garlic, and stir together to make a paste.

SALT AND PEPPER MARTINI ONIONS

ABOUT 1½ CUPS

2 cups mixed pearl onions, yellow, white, and purple

1 cup dry vermouth

1½ teaspoons freshly ground black pepper

½ teaspoon kosher salt

No need to worry about the splash of vermouth in your martini. It comes along with these tasty little onions.

Bring a saucepan filled with water to a boil. Add the onions and boil for 2 to 3 minutes. Drain in a colander and place under cold running water until cool. Peel off the skins.

Pour the vermouth into a measuring cup and stir in the black pepper and kosher salt. Place the onions in a jar, pour in the seasoned vermouth, cap tightly, and refrigerate. The onions will keep for up to 1 month, as long as they remain covered with vermouth.

SALT AND PEPPER CANDIED PECANS

1½ CUPS

2 tablespoons sugar

2 tablespoons maple syrup

1 teaspoon fine sea salt

½ teaspoon freshly ground black pepper

⅛ teaspoon cayenne pepper (optional)

1½ cups pecan halves

From roasted butternut squash soup and green salad to ice cream, cake, and crêpes, these spicy nuts are a great addition to your favorite dishes.

Preheat the oven to 325°F.

In a bowl, mix together the sugar, maple syrup, sea salt, black pepper, and cayenne, if using. Toss the pecan halves in the mixture to coat evenly, then spread on a nonstick baking sheet.

Bake the pecans for 5 minutes; stir them to make sure they are not sticking together. Bake for 8 to 10 minutes longer. The nuts will have taken on a golden tone. Let cool, then store in an airtight container at room temperature for up to 2 to 3 weeks.

PICKLED BEANS
AND LEEKS

1 cup rice vinegar

1 cup water

⅓ cup white wine
vinegar

2½ teaspoons kosher salt

1 tablespoon sugar

3 or 4 long peppers, or
8 black peppercorns

1 teaspoon
mustard seed

1 teaspoon
coriander seed

2 small leeks

¾ pound green beans,
trimmed

Here is a quick pickling method for green beans and leeks. You can enjoy these the day after you make them. You can also change the flavor by adding other seasonings, such as dill, thyme, rosemary, or even a chili pepper for a little heat. Serve them as part of an antipasto, or with picnic foods.

To make the pickling brine, in a nonreactive saucepan, combine the rice vinegar, water, wine vinegar, kosher salt, sugar, long peppers or peppercorns, mustard seed, and coriander seed. Bring to a simmer, then let cool.

Trim the leeks to the length of the beans, trim off the root ends, remove the tough outer leaves, and then slit lengthwise and rinse well under running cold water. Cut the leeks lengthwise into ½-inch-wide strips.

In a large sauté pan, pour in water to a depth of about 2 inches and bring to a boil. Add the green beans and leeks and cook, uncovered, until tender, 3 to 4 minutes. Drain well and stand the leeks and beans upright in glass canning jars with 2-part lids, or with glass lids with wire bales. The vegetables should fit snugly in quart jars. Pour in the pickling brine—the vegetables should be fully immersed in the liquid—and tightly cover the jars.

Refrigerate overnight before serving. The vegetables will keep for up to 2 weeks in the refrigerator.

GRAVLAX-STYLE HALIBUT

1 halibut fillet, about
  2 pounds, skinned

½ cup sugar

½ cup kosher salt

¼ cup lemon- or orange-
  flavored vodka

1 teaspoon freshly
  ground white pepper

2 large fresh dill sprigs,
  plus 2 tablespoons
  chopped

Mildly flavored and smooth textured, gravlax, a Swedish specialty, is relatively easy to make at home. Here, halibut replaces the traditional salmon. For an elegant appetizer, serve the cured fish in slices with paper-thin radish slices, thinly sliced pumpernickel bread, and a sauce of sour cream flavored with mustard.

Rinse the halibut fillet, pat dry, and place on a platter. In a small bowl, stir together the sugar and kosher salt until well mixed. Rub each side of the halibut fillet with half of the sugar-salt mixture. Then rub the vodka on each side, sprinkle both sides with the white pepper, and press 1 sprig of dill onto each side. Place the fillet in a large, zippered plastic bag, press out any air from the bag, and seal closed. Place the bag on a small baking sheet. Top with a plate or platter, and put a brick or large cans on top, to create about 5 pounds of weight. Refrigerate for 24 hours.

Just before serving, remove the fillet from the bag, discard the dill sprigs, and wipe off the excess moisture. Slice about ⅛ inch thick, sprinkle with the chopped dill, and serve.

ROASTED GARNET SWEET POTATOES

SERVES 4

2 large garnet sweet potatoes, about 1 pound total weight, peeled and cut into 1- to 2-inch chunks

2 tablespoons balsamic vinegar

3 shallots, quartered lengthwise

5 fresh thyme sprigs

1½ teaspoons freshly ground black pepper

1 teaspoon kosher salt

1 tablespoon unsalted butter, melted

1 tablespoon extra-virgin olive oil

Sweet potatoes or yams? What you are most likely seeing in your local store are sweet potatoes, even though the sign may say YAMS. True yams, tubers of a tropical vine, are typically grown in the West Indies, South America, Africa, and parts of Asia and are rarely seen in stores in the United States. Years ago, the garnet sweet potato, which has dark, thick skin, red-orange flesh, and a moist texture, underwent a name change to yam to distinguish it from its pale yellow, starchier, less sweet kin.

Preheat the oven to 400°F.

In a small baking dish, toss together all the ingredients. Roast the potatoes for 25 minutes, then stir them well. Continue to roast until the potatoes are tender when pierced with a fork, about 20 minutes longer. Serve warm.

SPOON BREAD

SERVES 4 TO 6

1 cup cooked white rice

1 cup grated parmesan cheese

¼ cup yellow cornmeal

2 cups buttermilk

2 eggs, beaten

2 tablespoons unsalted butter, melted

1 tablespoon chopped fresh sage

1 tablespoon freshly cracked black pepper

½ teaspoon kosher salt

½ teaspoon baking soda

1 teaspoon fine sea salt

This is a crusty, savory, very substantial side dish to accompany pot roast, roast chicken, or grilled fish. It can also be served as a meatless main dish with a glass of nice wine and a light salad to keep it good company.

Preheat the oven to 325°F. Butter a shallow, 1½-quart baking dish.

In a large bowl, combine all the ingredients except the sea salt. Mix well and pour into the prepared dish. Bake until the surface is crusty and golden, about 1 hour.

Sprinkle the dish with the sea salt as soon as it is removed from the oven, then serve hot.

ROASTED
TOMATO SOUP

2 cans (28 ounces
each) plum (roma)
tomatoes, drained

5 shallots, coarsely
chopped

½ teaspoon kosher salt

2 cups chicken broth

1 cup milk

1 teaspoon freshly
ground black pepper,
plus extra pepper
for serving

fine sea salt to taste

Winter is when nearly everyone begins to crave soups. Unfortunately, it is not the best time for cooking with fresh tomatoes. This rich and delicious soup calls for canned tomatoes, however, made more flavorful with the addition of a good dose of kosher salt and some time in the oven. Old-fashioned grilled cheese sandwiches pair perfectly with the soup.

Preheat the oven to 350°F.

Squeeze the tomatoes gently to release any seeds, then lay them in a single layer on a nonstick baking sheet. Sprinkle the shallots and kosher salt evenly over the tomatoes. Roast the tomatoes in the oven until soft and bubbling, about 45 minutes.

In a saucepan, combine the roasted tomatoes and shallots with the broth and place over medium heat. Bring to a simmer, stirring to combine, then remove from the heat. Let cool slightly, then, working in batches if necessary, pour into a food processor or blender and process until smooth. Return the purée to the pan over medium heat and reheat. Add the milk and the 1 teaspoon black pepper, stir well, and heat to serving temperature.

Ladle into warmed bowls and pass sea salt and additional pepper at the table.

SALT AND PEPPER FOCACCIA

THIS SAVORY FOCACCIA, WITH
ITS TOPPING OF THINLY SLICED
POTATOES, FRESHLY CRACKED
PEPPER, AND ROSEMARY SALT, CAN
BE SERVED ON ITS OWN AS A
LIGHT MEAL, SLICED IN HALF
HORIZONTALLY AND FILLED FOR
PANINI, OR CUT INTO CUBES
AND USED TO MAKE PANZANELLA,
THE ITALIAN BREAD SALAD.

SALT AND PEPPER FOCACCIA

1 packet (2½ teaspoons) active dry yeast

1 cup warm water

3½ cups all-purpose flour

1 teaspoon kosher salt

1 tablespoon freshly cracked black pepper

2 tablespoons extra-virgin olive oil

2 yukon gold potatoes, about ½ pound total weight, sliced about ⅛ inch thick

½ small red onion, sliced about ⅛ inch thick

1 tablespoon rosemary salt (page 16)

With a small salad, this bread makes a satisfying light meal. If you like cheese, sprinkle the focaccia with a little Parmesan before you slip it in the oven.

In a small bowl, sprinkle the yeast over the warm water and let stand until foamy, about 5 minutes. In a large bowl, stir together the flour, kosher salt, and black pepper. Add the yeast mixture to the flour mixture a little at a time, mixing well with a wooden spoon until the dough begins to hold together. Shape into a ball and transfer to a lightly floured work surface. Knead the dough until it is smooth and elastic, 5 to 10 minutes. Shape the dough into a ball, place in a large lightly oiled bowl, cover, and allow the dough to rise in a warm place until it is double in bulk, about 1 hour.

Preheat the oven to 400°F. Lightly oil a large baking sheet.

Turn the dough out onto the baking sheet and, using your fingers, press it out evenly to about 1 inch thick. It will not quite fill the pan. Brush the dough with the olive oil and allow it to stand for another 10 minutes. Arrange the potato slices evenly over the dough, then sprinkle the onion slices and the rosemary salt evenly over the potatoes.

Bake the focaccia until the edges are firm and golden, 20 to 25 minutes. Remove from the oven and slide the focaccia onto a cutting board. Cut into 12 pieces and serve warm.

GRILLED PORTOBELLO MUSHROOM PANINI

4 large portobello mushrooms

1 tablespoon fresh thyme leaves, chopped

1 teaspoon coarse sea salt

1½ teaspoons freshly ground black pepper

½ cup extra-virgin olive oil

4 sandwich rolls, split

1½ cups finely shredded gruyère cheese

salt and pepper garlic paste (page 97)

A grilled portobello mushroom and melted Gruyère sandwiched between the halves of a crusty roll might just replace your occasional craving for a burger. Flavorful and smoothly textured, the mushrooms, seasoned with sea salt, pepper, and thyme, cook quickly and benefit from the smokiness the charcoal imparts. The grilled portobellos can also be sliced and served over greens.

Prepare a hot fire in a grill.

Brush any dirt from the mushrooms with a damp cloth and remove the stems. Using the tip of a sharp knife, make small slits in each cap that are ¼ to ½ inch deep and ½ inch long, and that radiate from the center. As you make the slits, rock your knife from side to side so the slits are wide enough to hold some seasoning. In a small bowl, combine the thyme, sea salt, black pepper, and olive oil. Rub the thyme mixture onto the top of each mushroom, making sure the small slits are filled.

Place the mushrooms, gill side down, on the grill rack and grill for 2 minutes. Turn them over and grill for another 2 minutes. The mushrooms should be browned, softened, and have grill marks. Transfer the mushrooms to a paper or cloth towel to rest while you prepare the rolls.

Sprinkle the cut side of one-half of each roll with one-fourth of the cheese. Spread the other half of each roll with the garlic spread. Slice the mushrooms about ¼ inch thick, and lay the slices over the cheese. Replace the roll tops. One at a time, place the sandwiches in a sandwich press until the cheese melts. If you do not have a sandwich press, use a dry skillet over medium-high heat and a second, heavy skillet to weight the top.

Cut the sandwiches in half and serve warm.

SALT AND PEPPER CARBONARA

4 quarts water

¼ cup extra-virgin olive oil

4 cloves garlic, finely minced

¾ cup dry white wine

3 eggs

1 cup grated parmigiano-reggiano cheese

2 tablespoons kosher salt

1 pound spaghetti

1½ teaspoons freshly ground black pepper

We came up with this recipe while trying to create a pasta to feed our vegetarian friends. It is a variation of the traditional spaghetti alla carbonara, which combines eggs, cheese, pancetta, and sometimes a little cream.

In a large pot, bring the water to a rolling boil. While the water is heating, in a large skillet, heat the olive oil over medium-high heat. Add the garlic and sauté until it turns golden and becomes fragrant, 1 to 2 minutes. Slowly pour in the wine and cook until slightly reduced, 5 to 7 minutes. Remove from the heat and keep hot. In a small bowl, beat together the eggs and cheese.

When the water reaches a boil, add 1 tablespoon of the kosher salt, stir, and add the pasta. Cook the pasta, stirring occasionally to keep it from sticking together, until al dente, about 10 minutes. Using tongs, transfer the pasta to the skillet holding the wine and garlic. (Don't worry about the pasta water that comes along with the pasta, as it will add a bit of flavor and keep the pasta from being too dry.) Toss the pasta gently to coat it with the wine and garlic. Add the egg-cheese mixture, the remaining 1 tablespoon kosher salt, and the black pepper, and toss gently until pasta is evenly coated. The heat of the pasta will cook the eggs.

Transfer to a warmed pasta bowl and serve immediately.

CHICKEN-APPLE SAUSAGES

WITH SAUTÉED GRAPES

1 tablespoon extra-virgin olive oil

4 smoked chicken-apple sausages

1 shallot, finely chopped

2 cups mixed seedless grapes, coarsely chopped or left whole if small

1 teaspoon freshly ground black pepper

¼ teaspoon coarse sea salt

¼ teaspoon chopped fresh rosemary

½ cup dry red wine

2 teaspoons honey

Sweet and smoky, this Italian-inspired dish calls for flavorful, juicy grapes for the best result. Look for them in the market in late summer or early fall. Serve the sausages and grapes with crusty bread or over pasta.

In a sauté pan, heat the olive oil over medium-high heat. Add the sausages, shallot, and grapes and cook, shaking the pan occasionally so the sausages and grapes roll over to ensure even browning. When the shallot begins to brown, after about 2 minutes, the grapes should begin to lose some of their juice. Then add the black pepper, sea salt, rosemary, wine, and honey to the pan and cook, stirring, for 1 to 2 minutes longer. The sausages should be brown on all sides and heated through and the grapes should be pale, split, and collapsed.

Transfer to a serving dish and serve warm.

TURKEY SCALLOPINI

1 to 1¼ pounds boneless turkey breast

1 cup all-purpose flour

1 teaspoon kosher salt

2 tablespoons extra-virgin olive oil, plus 1 tablespoon if needed

3 tablespoons unsalted butter

2 cloves garlic, minced

⅓ cup capers

1½ cups dry white wine

2 tablespoons fresh lemon juice

2 tablespoons lemon pepper (page 52)

¾ cup chopped fresh flat-leaf (italian) parsley

The combination of lemon and pepper brings a pleasantly piquant flavor to this dish. Pass more of the seasoned pepper at the table for those who want extra heat. When mincing the garlic, try sprinkling a little wine on the cutting board and on your knife blade. It will keep the garlic from sticking and make it easier to mince.

Slice the turkey against the grain into ½-inch-thick rounds. You should have 8 to 10 slices. Lightly pound each slice to flatten evenly to about ¼ inch thick. Mix together the flour and kosher salt on a plate. Dust each turkey slice on both sides with the flour mixture, shaking off the excess.

In a large sauté pan, heat 2 tablespoons each olive oil and butter over medium-high heat. When hot, add half of the turkey slices, being careful not to crowd the pan. As each slice turns gold to light brown on the bottom, after about 2 minutes, turn it over and cook the other side until golden, about 2 minutes longer. The turkey pieces should be firm to the touch. Remove to a warmed platter. Add the remaining turkey slices and cook the same way; keep warm.

Add the garlic and capers to the pan over medium-high heat (you may need an extra tablespoon of olive oil at this point), and as the garlic begins to turn golden, add the white wine. Scrape up any browned bits from the bottom of the pan and stir them into the sauce. Cook for 2 minutes, then add the remaining 1 tablespoon butter, the lemon juice, the lemon pepper, and the parsley, and stir until the butter melts.

Pour the sauce over the turkey slices and serve at once.

TURKEY JERKY

2 tablespoons
kosher salt

1 tablespoon
brown sugar

1 teaspoon peeled and
chopped fresh ginger

½ teaspoon freshly
ground black pepper

2 cloves garlic, crushed

2 tablespoons light
soy sauce

1½ cups pineapple juice

1 pound boneless
turkey breast, cut into
long, thin strips about
¼ inch wide

Custom-made dried turkey strips, or jerky, are more tender and much more flavorful than any you buy at the store. They are great for travel, very low in fat, and can be made to your desired level of spiciness with the addition of more ground pepper to the marinade.

In a bowl, combine all the ingredients except the turkey and mix well. Add the turkey strips and turn them to coat evenly. Place the turkey strips and marinade in a large, zippered plastic bag, press out any air from the bag, and seal closed. Refrigerate for 24 hours, picking up the bag once or twice during that time to redistribute the marinade.

Preheat the oven to 250°F.

Remove the turkey strips from the marinade, drain well, and lay them on a wire rack placed on top of a baking sheet lined with aluminum foil. Bake the strips, turning once, until brown and leathery, 3½ to 4 hours. Let cool completely, then place in a zippered plastic bag or tightly capped jar. Store in the refrigerator for up to 3 weeks.

PEPPERED POT ROAST

1 boneless chuck roast, 3 to 3½ pounds

3 to 4 tablespoons cumin, salt, and pepper (page 97)

1 bunch green onions, including tender green tops, cut into 3-inch lengths

¼ cup dry red wine

This roast is slow cooked, savory, and incredibly simple to assemble, and it will make your home smell great for the hours it is in the oven. Because it is wrapped in foil, it is also very easy to clean up. When the roast is done, it will be tender and nearly moist enough to spread. Serve slices of it over wide noodles or mashed potatoes, or place slices on warm corn tortillas, top with your favorite salsa, and roll up.

Preheat the oven to 350°F.

Use a piece of aluminum foil large enough to enclose the roast. (You may need to cut the roast in half and make 2 foil packets if your roast is too large or if your foil is not wide enough.) Lay the roast on the foil and sprinkle half of the cumin mixture over it. Rub the spices into the meat a bit. Turn the roast over and sprinkle the other half of the cumin mixture over it. Again, rub it into the meat. Scatter the green onions over the top of the roast. Bring up the sides of the foil to create a bowl shape, and pour the wine over the roast. Fold the edges of the foil together and crimp tightly to form a secure packet.

Place the foil packet in the oven and roast for 2 hours. Remove it from the oven, open the foil, turn the roast over, recrimp the foil closed, and roast for 2 hours longer. The roast will be fork-tender.

Unwrap the roast, place it on a warmed platter, and let rest for about 5 minutes before slicing. Serve warm.

SPICY AND CRISP, FRIED FRESH SAGE LEAVES ARE AN IRRESISTIBLE APPETIZER; SERVE THEM AS IS, OR WITH A DIPPING SAUCE. USE THEM WHOLE OR CRUSHED AS A GARNISH FOR DISHES SUCH AS MEATS, GRATINS, OR PASTAS.

SALT AND PEPPER FRIED SAGE LEAVES

SALT AND PEPPER
FRIED SAGE LEAVES

20 large fresh sage
leaves, stems
removed

1 cup dry white wine

1 tablespoon
rice vinegar

⅓ cup cornstarch

⅓ cup all-purpose flour

¼ teaspoon kosher salt

¼ teaspoon freshly
ground black pepper

¼ teaspoon
ground cumin

vegetable oil
for frying

fleur de sel
to taste

Serve these aromatic, crunchy leaves as a snack or use as a condiment on roast pork, pork chops, or roast chicken, or to garnish soups. Each crisp leaf delivers a simple combination of salt and heat.

Place the sage leaves in a small bowl. Pour the wine and vinegar over them and allow to stand at room temperature for at least 30 minutes or for up to 1 hour.

In a small, shallow bowl, stir together the cornstarch, flour, kosher salt, black pepper, and cumin. Remove the leaves from the wine mixture and, while they are still damp, coat each leaf with the flour mixture, pressing lightly so that the dusting adheres to the leaf. Set aside on a plate.

Line a plate with paper towels and set aside.

Pour vegetable oil to a depth of ½ inch into a sauté pan and heat over medium-high heat until the oil shimmers but is not smoking. Working in batches of 5 or 6 leaves, drop the leaves into the oil. As soon as they begin to turn golden, turn each leaf once. The total frying time should be about 1 minute. Using a slotted spoon, transfer the leaves to the prepared plate to drain. They can be kept hot in a warm oven for up to 30 minutes.

Just before serving, sprinkle the leaves generously with fleur de sel. Serve hot.

ROAST CHICKEN

2½ gallons water

1 cup sugar

2 cups kosher salt

1 tablespoon black peppercorns, cracked

1 tablespoon white peppercorns, cracked

1 tablespoon dried green peppercorns, cracked

1 head garlic, cloves separated and peeled

2 roasting chickens, 3½ to 4 pounds each

2 bunches fresh thyme

2 tablespoons extra-virgin olive oil

2 teaspoons freshly ground black pepper

1 lemon, cut in half

Brining the chicken overnight ensures a moist, juicy, perfectly seasoned bird. This brine works equally well with a whole turkey.

In large container, combine the water, sugar, kosher salt, all the peppercorns, and the garlic cloves and stir to dissolve the salt and sugar. Rinse the chickens and place each in a large pot or other container. Pour half of the brine mixture over each chicken. Divide 1 thyme bunch in half and add to each batch of brine. If necessary, weight down each chicken with a bowl or plate to keep it fully immersed in the brine. Cover and refrigerate overnight or for up to 24 hours. Bring to room temperature before proceeding.

Preheat the oven to 350°F.

Remove each chicken from the brine, rinse well, and pat dry. Place the chickens on a baking sheet lined with aluminum foil. Rub each chicken all over with 1 tablespoon of the olive oil and 1 teaspoon of the ground black pepper. Fill each chicken cavity with a lemon half and the remaining thyme.

Place the chickens in the oven and roast for 1½ hours. To test for doneness, insert an instant-read thermometer in the thickest part of the thigh away from the bone; it will register 175°F when the chicken is ready. Alternatively, pierce the thigh joint with the tip of a knife; the juices should run clear.

Transfer the chickens to warmed platters, tent with aluminum foil, and let rest for 15 to 20 minutes before carving.

SALT-ROASTED PEARS
WITH CAMEMBERT

4 firm but ripe bartlett, packham, or anjou pears

4 pounds rock salt

2 tablespoons hazelnut liqueur

¼ pound camembert cheese

freshly ground black pepper to taste

Salt-roasting pears makes the skins slightly salty and a bit crisp. You can prep the pears in advance, and then place them in the oven right before you sit down to dinner or halfway through the meal.

Preheat the oven to 350°F.

Holding a paring knife at a 45-degree angle, cut out a 1-inch round from the bottom of each pear. Save the rounds to cap the pears later. With a melon baller or a small spoon, remove the seeds and core. If possible, leave the stems of the pears intact for presentation.

Pour the rock salt into an ovenproof pot. Place the pears, stem side down, in the salt, nesting them in so that they are about two-thirds covered. Place ½ tablespoon of the liqueur in each pear cavity. Cut the Camembert into 4 equal pieces and place 1 piece in each cavity. Replace the small round on the bottom of each pear.

Roast the pears in the oven for 1 hour. They should be browned on the outside and feel soft when lightly squeezed. If they are still too firm, return them to the oven for 10 to 15 minutes longer.

To serve, remove the pears from the salt and brush off any remaining crystals. Place each pear in a bowl or on a dessert plate, slice, and serve immediately. Pass the black pepper at the table.

SALTED TANGERINE SECTIONS

WITH PEPPER DIPPING SAUCE

½ cup water

2 tablespoons kosher salt

4 tangerines, peeled, sectioned, and all pith removed

1½ tablespoons freshly ground black pepper

2 tablespoons fresh tangerine juice

These fruit bites are a light and satisfying finish to a meal. The pepper sauce adds spice to the palate-pleasing combination of salty and sweet. Or you can serve them plain with other nibbles or appetizers at a cocktail party.

In a small bowl, stir together the water and kosher salt until the salt dissolves. Place the tangerine sections in the bowl and toss to coat with the salted water. Lay the sections on a wire rack for several hours until they are dry and their skins are tight.

In a small bowl, stir together the black pepper and tangerine juice. Transfer to a dipping bowl.

Serve the tangerine sections at room temperature with the dipping sauce.

BAKER'S CATALOGUE

Tel: 800.827.6836

Web site:

bakerscatalogue.com

Fleur de sel, kosher, gray
Celtic, and Maldon salts,
plus several other varieties
of French sea salt, both
fine and coarse; also sour
salt. Catalogue available.

CHEFSHOP.COM

Tel: 877.337.2491

Web site: chefshop.com
French, Italian and
Sicilian, and New Zealand
sea salts; Halen Môn sea
salt; fleur de sel; sea salt
and herb blends; Hawaiian
alae salt; Tellicherry and
Szechuan peppercorns.

**COOKING SCHOOL
OF ASPEN**

414 East Hyman Avenue
Aspen, CO 81611
Tel: 800.603.6004
Smoked Danish salt and
Peruvian pink salt.

CORTI BROTHERS

5810 Folsom Boulevard
Sacramento, CA
95819-4610
Tel: 916.736.3800
Oshima Island and
Trapani salts.

DEAN & DELUCA

Tel: 800.221.7714

Web site: deandeluca.com
Ile de Ré fleur de sel; Sea
Star brand French sea
salt; Hawaiian alae salt;
pink, green, white, and
Tellicherry peppercorns.
Catalogue available.

FINE FEAST GOURMET

Tel: 877.788.2295

Web site: fine-feast.com
Trapani sea salt, four-
pepper blend.

HAWAII KAI SALTS

Tel: 808.553.3461

Hawaiian black lava and
alae salts; also Hawaiian
smoked kai salt.

PENZEYS SPICES

Tel: 800.741.7787

Web site: penzeys.com
Malabar, Sarawak, Muntok,
and Tellicherry pepper-
corns. Catalogue available.

THE SPICE HOUSE

Web site:

thespicehouse.com
Szechuan, Lampong black,
Muntok white, Mysore
green, and Réunion pink
peppercorns.

WILLIAMS-SONOMA

Tel: 800.541.2233

Web site:

williams-sonoma.com
Ile de Ré fleur de sel,
five-pepper blend
(includes allspice), salt
and pepper grinders.
Catalogue available.

ZINGERMAN'S

Tel: 888.636.8162

Web site: zingermans.com
Maldon, Celtic gray,
Sicilian, and Halen
Môn sea salts. Catalogue
available.

BIBLIOGRAPHY

CLINGERMAN, POLLY. *The Kitchen Companion: The Ultimate Guide to Cooking and the Kitchen.* Gaithersburg, Maryland: The American Cooking Guild, 1994.

DAVIDSON, ALAN. *The Oxford Companion to Food.* New York: Oxford University Press, 1999.

ELKORT, MARTIN. *The Secret Life of Food: A Feast of Food and Drink History, Folklore, and Fact.* Los Angeles: Jeremy P. Tarcher, 1991.

HILLMAN, HOWARD. *Kitchen Science: A Guide to Knowing the Hows and Whys for Fun and Success in the Kitchen.* Rev. ed. Boston: Houghton Mifflin Company, 1989.

JORDAN, MICHELE ANNA. *Salt and Pepper: 135 Perfectly Seasoned Recipes.* New York: Broadway Books, 1999.

KURLANSKY, MARK. *Salt: A World History.* New York: Walker & Company, 2002.

LASZLO, PIERRE. *Salt: Grain of Life.* Translated by Mary Beth Mader. New York: Columbia University Press, 2001.

MCGEE, HAROLD. *On Food and Cooking: The Science and Lore of the Kitchen.* New York: Charles Scribner's Sons, 1984.

NORMAN, JILL. *The Burns Philp Book of Spices.* London: Dorling Kindersley, 1990. Special ed., reprinted for Burns, Philp & Company in Australia, 1995.

TANNAHILL, REAY. *Food in History.* New York: Three Rivers Press, 1988.

TISDALE, SALLY. *Lot's Wife: Salt and the Human Condition.* New York: Henry Holt & Company, 1988.

VISSER, MARGARET. *Much Depends on Dinner: The Extraordinary History and Mythology, Allure and Obsessions, Perils and Taboos of an Ordinary Meal.* New York: Grove Press, 1986.

WILLIAMS, CHUCK, ED. *Williams-Sonoma Kitchen Companion: The A to Z Guide to Everyday Cooking Equipment and Ingredients.* New York: Time-Life Books, 2000.

ACKNOWLEDGMENTS

There is an old superstition: If you spill salt it's bad luck, and you must throw some over your shoulder to transform the bad luck into good. Clearly we tossed a lot of salt over our collective shoulders in making this book to receive so much good fortune during the process. The extraordinary people who accompanied us through this journey effected a huge amount of our luck.

We thank Louise Fili and Mary Jane Callister for their ability to read our minds and surpass our expectations, delivering a most beautiful book. And to the staff of Louise Fili Ltd., Jessica Disbrow and Melissa Jun, thanks for all your effort.

We thank Carolyn Miller for delving into these subjects with her usual precision, humor, clarity, and poetry.

We thank our agent Liv Blumer for her unstinting patience, guidance and support.

We thank Bill LeBlond and Sara Schneider at Chronicle Books for their ongoing partnership.

We thank photo assistants Jeri Jones and Heidi Ladendorf for leaping over the bar gracefully and smartly no matter how high we set it.

We thank Elisabet derNederlander, Ann Tonai, Michelle Repine, and Vicki Roberts for testing, tasting, and fine tuning recipes throughout the project.

We thank Bob and his staff at Mission Market in San Francisco for their beautiful fish, poultry, and generosity.

And we especially thank our families—Melanie and Isabel, Janet and Kendall, Mark, Katie, Sybil and David—for their love and patience.

The exact equivalents in the following tables have been rounded for convenience.

LIQUID/DRY MEASURES

U.S.	METRIC
¼ teaspoon	1.25 milliliters
½ teaspoon	2.5 milliliters
1 teaspoon	5 milliliters
1 tablespoon (3 teaspoons)	15 milliliters
1 fluid ounce (2 tablespoons)	30 milliliters
¼ cup	60 milliliters
⅓ cup	80 milliliters
½ cup	120 milliliters
1 cup	240 milliliters
1 pint (2 cups)	480 milliliters
1 quart (4 cups, 32 ounces)	960 milliliters
1 gallon (4 quarts)	3.84 liters
1 ounce (by weight)	28 grams
1 pound	454 grams
2.2 pounds	1 kilogram

LENGTH

U.S.	METRIC
⅛ inch	3 millimeters
¼ inch	6 millimeters
½ inch	12 millimeters
1 inch	2.5 centimeters

OVEN TEMPERATURE

FAHRENHEIT	CELSIUS	GAS
250	120	½
275	140	1
300	150	2
325	160	3
350	180	4
375	190	5
400	200	6
425	220	7
450	230	8
475	240	9
500	260	10